more

FORGOTTEN SKILLS

of SELF-SUFFICIENCY

more
FORGOTTEN
SKILLS

of SELF-SUFFICIENCY

CALEB WARNOCK

HOBBLE CREEK PRESS

AN IMPRINT OF CEDAR FORT, INC.
SPRINGVILLE, UTAH

ISBN 13: 978-1-4621-1343-9

Published by Hobble Creek Press, an imprint of Cedar Fort, Inc.
2373 W. 700 S., Springville, UT 84663
Distributed by Cedar Fort, Inc., www.cedarfort.com

LIBRARY OF CONGRESS CATALOGING-IN-PUBLICATION DATA

Warnock, Caleb (Caleb J.), 1973-
More forgotten skills of self-sufficiency / Caleb Warnock.
    pages cm
Includes bibliographical references and index.
ISBN 978-1-4621-1343-9
1. Self-reliant living--Handbooks, manuals, etc. I. Title.
GF78.W373 2014
640--dc23
                              2013039187

Cover and page design by Erica Dixon
Cover design © 2014 by Lyle Mortimer
Edited by Casey J. Winters

Printed in The United States of America

10 9 8 7 6 5 4 3 2 1

TO MY ETERNAL MIG:

Everything we have—
hard-won, long in coming, bright and new—
will one day give way to entropy and
disappear.

Not us. We go on
beyond this world.

We're just beginning a good run.

CONTENTS

A wheat horde more than 40 years old.

CHAPTER 1
STOP BEING PREPARED

Since my first book arrived on shelves, I have given presentations, demonstrations, and speeches to thousands of people. The biggest lesson I have learned from these experiences is that people have confused self-sufficiency for preparedness.

After fielding thousands of emails and thousands of questions, I have become convinced that the desire to be a "prepper" has gotten hugely in the way of our ability to be self-sufficient. Preparedness has become a distraction that is actually defeating our goal of self-reliance. I don't say this casually because I think the desire to be prepared for emergencies is good—but not if it becomes a stumbling block toward our self-sufficiency.

The goals of preparedness are entirely different from the goals of self-reliance. Let's look at some examples:

The prepared family:	The self-reliant family:
1. Spends big money to purchase a stockpile of dried, canned food.	1. Eats fresh, free, and nutritious homegrown food 365 days a year.
2. Stockpiles medicines and health products against future need.	2. Uses backyard natural herbal health treatments as a first-line defense.
3. Rarely relies on their prepared, processed bulk food for everyday eating (be honest, now!)	3. Uses cash saved by avoiding the grocery store (as much as possible) for necessities and luxuries (starting with debt reduction).
4. Plans to use part of their purchased stockpile to barter for necessities if the need arises in a crisis.	4. Barters with homemade and homegrown items.

These days, my advice to families everywhere is to stop being prepared and start being self-sufficient.

HERE'S WHY:

Do you really plan to live off freeze-dried food and canned powders?

I was giving a speech to a preparedness group recently, talking about eating fresh from the winter garden, when a woman in the audience raised her hand with a confused look on her face. "You don't buy bulk food?" she asked. "You can really eat from your garden in winter—enough to feed your family?"

"Yes, yes, yes," I said.

She didn't look convinced. "Really?"

"Not only is my answer yes, but I'll tell you something else," I volunteered. "If I had to eat freeze-dried food and oddly-colored powders from cans for the rest of my life, I'd run toward the crisis—whatever it was—and not away from it. Yuck. I like to eat too much to live on that stuff."

I wasn't kidding.

Let's go back to my original question: Do you really plan to live off bulk and freeze-dried food? Your answer is a resounding no, and I can prove it to you—because you aren't eating your food storage now.

Yesterday afternoon, as I write this, I was sitting in my home office working when the phone rang. It was one of my neighbors. He had cleaned out his garage and loaded more than one thousand pounds of food storage—wheat and beans—into the back of his truck. "I was getting ready to take it to the dump," he said, "and then I thought, you guys have chickens. I wonder if you could make use of this."

Salad picked fresh in December from the author's winter garden.

Um, yes! So he brought it over and we unloaded it in my garage. A few minutes later, he came back with more. He was happy to be rid of it, and my wife and I were thrilled to have it as chicken food.

How much do you think he spent on all that stuff that he gave us? How long has it been taking up space in his garage? And here is the real question: Why hasn't his family eaten it?

Because they don't want to.

Be honest with yourself, now. If you are reading this book, you are probably interested in preparedness. How much have you spent on freeze-dried bulk foods since you were married? And how much of it have you used? Can you even remember the last time someone in your house opened up one of those cans to make something for dinner?

And yet, we buy this stuff, spending thousands of our hard-earned dollars, because it makes us feel prepared. All evidence to the contrary.

My suggestion is this: If we're spending a lot of money on cans, and we are not using it, perhaps it's time to consider a new option.

CHAPTER 2

THE FUTURIST: "I DON'T CARE ABOUT YOU"

Not long ago, I was asked to speak to a church group. I give this speech a lot, and as a rule, about halfway through, I take out a yellowing, folded piece of paper, unfold it to reveal the inside, and ask if anyone knows what it is. This paper is one of the most important, meaningful, and emotional pieces of paper in United States history. Take a look at the picture on page 5, and I'll pose the same question to you. Do you know what it is?

Almost always, no one does.

But on this occasion, there was a little old woman on the front row, and she piped right up.

"I know what that is," she said. "I lived that. That is a World War II ration book."

"You are in trouble," I said, disrespectfully wagging a finger at her face (she was in her eighties). "Answer me this: Have you told your children and your grandchildren about what it was like to live through years of rationing? Have you written it down?"

With honest eyes, she slowly shook her head. "We don't talk about it," she said. She looked a little startled, as if she had (rightfully) expected to be

held up as a hero for living through World War II. But I had something else in mind. I wanted to make a point.

"Your experience of living through World War II does no one any good if you are not teaching your grandchildren the lessons you learned. Lessons of self-reliance," I said bluntly.

She promised to go home and start talking to her loved ones. (We've since become friends and traded seeds, kefir, and other things.)

My ration book is not a copy; it is the genuine article. It is "War Ration Book One," issued in 1942. Mine has three of the original stamps still intact. In 1942, those three stamps could have been redeemed for a can of green beans. The book originally belonged to Albert and Lillian Dollenbacher of Cavour, Beadle County, South Dakota, according to the form inside the book. I purchased it at an antique store on the Oregon Coast and it has been to many, many speeches with me.

"We have been warned," I say in my presentations as I hold up the ration book for everyone to glimpse. "We have had to take care of ourselves before."

When a nation—even the strongest, wealthiest nation in the world—sends its troops to protect freedom half the globe over, the troops can't just stop at a restaurant when they get hungry or head over to Costco during a lull in the fighting. Nazi Germany didn't throw open the doors of their neighborhood grocery stores, believe it or not. We had 16.1 million fighting men and women to feed—and on average, they were abroad for sixteen months. We had to keep them from starving.

Problem was, there was very little metal for cans. In 1942, metal cans were the only option for shipping and safely storing food—whether the food was destined for the warfront, or headed to US grocery stores. Metal was in intensely short supply—we had to have metal to make tanks, planes, guns, and bullets. Here is a startling fact: we had enough metal to can food to feed the country, or feed the troops. Here is another fact: as a nation, we were able to produce enough food on farms to feed the people at home, or feed the troops abroad. We could not feed both.

Think about that for a moment. The families at home starve or the troops starve.

To solve the problem, a massive campaign to get Americans to grow gardens was launched. They were called "Victory Gardens." Any food you could grow, you did not need ration stamps and money to buy.

At the end of the war, the war department announced that Victory Gardeners had grown as much food in backyards, school playgrounds, and vacant lots as all of the farms combined. Without Victory Gardens, we would have lost the war.

Now ask yourself a few questions:

- In 1942, what percent of the adult population of America had a living knowledge of how to garden self-sufficiently? What do you think that percentage is today?

- In 1942, during the hardest of hard times, what percentage of the US population expected someone else—the government, neighbors, churches, extended family—to take care of them if they were struggling, whether by providing them food or cash to pay the light bill so they didn't have to provide it themselves? What do you think that percentage is today?

- In 1942, what percentage of US families do you think had debt? Today?

- In 1942, what percentage of the United States knew how to save seeds from their own backyard garden? Today?

- What percentage, in 1942, could honestly say they were living within their means? Had their mortgage paid off? Their car paid off? How about today?

Twenty million people starved to death in World War II in Europe. And we have not even talked about World War I.

In 1922, Fridtjof Nansen of Norway was awarded a Nobel Peace Prize. He is famous to the world for his pioneering exploration of the North

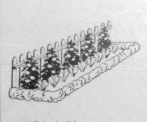

(top) Cover of World War II ration book. (bottom left) Three original stamps remain in the author's ration book. (bottom right) Inside page of a Victory Gardening guide.

Two wartime Victory Garden guides from the author's collection.

Pole and his global work to stop starvation during and after the First World War. He is famous to me for his work developing winter lettuces. His Nobel lecture should be read by everyone. One paragraph in particular is meaningful to me:

> I shall always remember a day in a village east of the Volga to which only one-third of its inhabitants had returned; of the remaining two-thirds, some had fled and the rest had died of starvation. Most of the animals had been slaughtered; but courage had still not been completely extinguished, and although their prospects were bleak, the people still had faith in the future. "Give us seed," they said, "and we will sow it in

Lettuce growing in winter in the author's unheated geothermal greenhouse. In the bottom left corner is the amazing winter lettuce called North Pole, now very rare, created by Fridtjof Nansen.

The author's 2-year-old granddaughter, Ada Mae, holding summer squash in the author's garden.

Conrad, the author's grandson, holding rare runner beans in the author's garden.

the soil." "Yes", we replied, "but what will you do without animals to pull the plough?" "That does not matter," they said; "if there are no animals, we will put ourselves and our women and children to the plough." It was not self-indulgence that was speaking here, not extravagance, not mere showmanship—it was the very will to stay alive, which had not given in.

Must we all live through the bitter pangs of hunger before we learn the real value of work?[1]

When I am speechifying (so to speak), after discussing the ration book, I like to say this: "Pay careful attention to what I'm about to say. This is the most important thing I have to share with you:

"I don't care about you."

I explain that the people who sit in the audience at my speeches are a lost cause. They will take the information I have given them and think about it for a day or two. But will they change? A year from my speech, will they be more self-reliant? If the answer is no, why am I wasting my time?

Because I *do* care about the children and the grandchildren. We have to change for them.

Here is what I know for sure: We need far more living examples of self-reliance today than we have.

At one point in 2010, about 40 percent of the homes in the extremely affluent town where I live were having their utility bills paid by The Church of Jesus Christ of Latter-day Saints out of funds "for the poor and needy" (as told in a local church talk).

Photo taken circa 1921 by the Fridtjof Nansen party in a war-torn village in Russia. Perhaps the most chilling picture of starvation ever taken. Much of the straw on the roof is missing because the people ate it for food. (Photo courtesy of the National Library of Norway's online database service.)

We are talking about people who, in some cases, had taken out debt for million-dollar homes. (My wife and I do not live in a million-dollar home, just to be clear. We live on the "poor side of town"—so called because we live where people have chickens!) I happen to know for a fact that some of those people, while having their utilities kept on with sacred funds, were eating dinner at McDonald's.

My grandparents and great-grandparents would have gone without eating long before they would have let anyone, let alone their church congregation, pay their utility bills.

What happened to the fires of personal pride and self-respect that once fueled Americans to proud self-reliance?

Today's generation is watching their parents and grandparents. This young generation is being taught the "fine art" of living off credit cards, of expecting the government or someone else to come to their rescue when times are tough. They might not have any savings, yet they have smartphones. Their parents might be paying their smartphone bills, but the kids have tickets for all the must-see blockbuster movies.

Remember the old woman I chastised during my speech? Afterward, she told me that her kids, working alongside their parents, put themselves through college by growing and selling strawberries from a field during summers.

I have some knowledge of self-reliance because my great-grandparents lived a self-reliant life everyday, and I was lucky enough to know them. My grandparents had huge gardens, not for show, but for feeding the kids and grandkids. My grandparents proudly lived within their means, no matter what that meant doing without.

It doesn't take a genius to read the tea leaves and see what is coming. Will your kids and grandkids see unbridled prosperity or hard times? Will they be prepared? Will they have learned self-reliance from you?

HERE IS WHAT THE FUTURE HOLDS:

You might think some of it harsh. I have used unvarnished words on purpose:

• **FAMILIES WHOSE PROPERTY RIGHTS** are legally restricted by the covenants, conditions and restrictions (CC&Rs) of a homeowners association will face an uphill battle when trying to increase their self-reliance through growing backyard vegetables, eggs, and meat. We know this for sure because this is already happening. Property burdened by CC&Rs will become an albatross around the necks of families looking to shift toward a healthier life, both financially and nutritionally.

• **FAMILIES WITH CREDIT CARD DEBT** and otherwise messy finances will suffer every time the price of gas hits a new record high. We know this because it is already happening.

• **FAMILIES THAT ARE FORCED TO RELY ON** the grocery store for food will find themselves playing Russian roulette with their health. According to new numbers from the US Centers for Disease Control, 48 million Americans are poisoned by grocery store and restaurant food each year.[2] The number of people poisoned by foodborne illnesses from mass-produced food that is grown, prepared, and shipped by low-wage workers will only continue to rise. We know this because it is happening all around us.

• **FOR THE AVERAGE FAMILY,** a larger and larger percentage of the budget will be out of the family's immediate control. This will be due to bad short-term decisions with long-term natural consequences: for example, borrowing to buy immodest, ornamented homes, cars, clothes, and vacations (which led church congregations to pay utility bills for financially underwater families in my town), coupled with inflation in the price of food, energy, insurance, and interest payments. We know this because we have begun

Fridtjof Nansen, center, was high commissioner for refugees and leader of the relief work for the starving in Russia. Here he is shown tasting the food that the homeless children received at a food station in November or December 1921 in rural Russia. (Photo courtesy of the National Library of Norway's online database service.)

to see it already (though only to a small degree at this writing).

• **CHILDREN WHO ARE BROUGHT UP** to think that recreation is done while sitting in front of an electronic device, instead of running, exploring, and getting dirty in a backyard, will grow up to be obese. This has already begun to happen.

• **CHILDREN WHO ARE TAUGHT TO EAT** the foods advertised in commercials on television will grow up obese and ill. This has already begun to happen.

• **CHILDREN WHO ARE NOT REQUIRED** to develop a work ethic before they leave home will grow up expecting someone to take care of them. This has already begun to happen.

• **PEOPLE WHO ARE OBESE AND ILL** because of their food decisions will not be available to serve their nation or their family during a time of need. Instead, they are likely to be a burden to nation and community.

• **LAST OF ALL, THIS:** Anyone over a certain age knows that children may not *appear* to be listening or watching, but when those children are grown up, they are likely to return to—or at least reexamine—the examples and practices of their parents and grandparents. Will we have prepared them with the skills and habits they will need in a tumultuous future? If they follow our example, will that be good or bad? Will they know how to be self-reliant because we showed them?

Notes

1. Nansen, "The Suffering People of Europe."

2. Centers for Disease Control and Prevention, "Estimates of Foodborne Illness in the United States."

CHAPTER 3

THE FUTURIST: GETTING WHAT YOU WANT

(INSTEAD OF FEARING YOU'LL GO WANTING)

Starting on a path to self-sufficiency begins by asking yourself one question: "What do I want?"

Too many of us have been asking the wrong question for a long time. We've been asking ourselves what we don't want. Or rather, people trying to sell us expensive "preparedness" stuff have been asking us this question. But the question is flawed.

In the world of sales, asking the customer to envision what they don't want is a method of motivating a purchase through fear—"If you don't want X, Y, or Z scary future, you need to buy A, B and C. If you don't buy now, you'll always regret being caught unprepared for the zombie apocalypse!"

I think we've had enough scare tactics.

The opposite of fear-based decision making is to decide what you want now, and in the future.

TRY SOME OF THESE ON FOR SIZE:

- "I want to spend less at the grocery store beginning now, which would give our family budget some breathing room to pay down our debts or pay extra on the mortgage."

- "I want to eat healthy to be healthy. I want the kids (or grandkids) to know what real, fresh, homegrown food tastes like—and how to grow it."

- "I want my family to have a living knowledge of self-reliance. They will be happier and more secure for it in the long run."

I wonder if we talk enough as families about what we want and why we want it. When I give presentations, I ask audiences to close their eyes and raise their hand if they have credit card debt. Or children with credit card debt. And then this: "Raise your hand if you don't know if your adult children have credit card debt because you've never talked about it."

The number of raised hands is always revealing.

If adult children have credit card debt, clearly that will be their responsibility and burden. But have you talked to them about what you want for them when it comes to debt? Have you talked to them about good and bad true-life examples of debt from your own life? I'm not talking about scolding or confronting or even demanding a confession from adult children. I'm not suggesting that you demand to know if they have debt, and if so, how much. And I'm not suggesting that you list your debts to your kids, if you have debts. What I am suggesting is simply talking about your goals, your accomplishments, and what you want for yourself and those you love. Talk to your spouse about your self-reliance goals. If appropriate, call a family meeting with the extended family. Here are some questions that can help your family gauge your level of self-reliance:

1. Did you eat anything in the past day that came from your own property instead of the grocery store? How about the past week? Month?

2. Over the past winter, did you store anything from your garden for your family to eat? For example, winter squash or potatoes or carrots? Did you use them?

3. Beginning right now, could you eat for the next week without going to the grocery store?

Will you take the challenge?

Once you establish how self-reliant you are now, the next step is to ask yourself how self-reliant you want to be, and when. List the steps necessary to get from where you are to where you want to be. Here are some suggestions:

If you have not grown a garden in the past year, but you have a garden space:

1. Plant a raspberry bush or three.

I always suggest this as a starting place, for several reasons. First, raspberry bushes are perennial, meaning they will grow and produce fruit for many years, which makes them easy. Second, I promise you the raspberries will get eaten. Third, I promise you that your kids or grandkids will always remember eating those fresh berries from your backyard. If this is the only memory of self-sufficiency you leave the next generations, at least you will have left them with the taste of real food in their mouths.

2. List the ten foods your family buys most.

If none of them are vegetables, you might want to rethink how your family eats. Decide which vegetables your family would really eat and start growing them. Lettuce, carrots, and corn are often favorites. Commit to growing a small garden, even if it is a four-foot by four-foot patch. Commit to pull a few weeds, to plant a few seeds, to keep an eye on the water. Growing only what you know your family will eat means your "starter" plan is rooted in reality.

3. List the five packaged foods you buy most.

Decide to replace those packaged foods in your diet with homegrown or locally grown food. Begin to wean your family from packaged food.

If you do not have garden space:

1. Borrow a garden.

When I was a college student, I went to a nearby elderly couple and introduced myself as their new neighbor. I explained to them where I was living, and that I wanted to grow a garden, and asked if I could borrow the neglected garden space in their backyard, along with access to a backyard hose and water tap. In exchange, I would share the garden produce with them half and half. They immediately and readily agreed, and for the next two years I used their garden space—and they were thrilled with the arrangement and so happy to see the land being productive and useful again. There are so many benefits to this option. First, you make friends with your neighbors. Second, an elderly couple who clearly at one point loved to grow fresh food gets fresh food again—I promise you they will be enormously grateful. Third, you get access to an established garden space with free water. Fourth, no money changes hands, no fees, no red tape—just neighborly goodwill. Everyone involved comes out a winner.

I was in college doing this long before the economy went sour, but these days, more and more people are getting into the spirit of borrowing a garden. I know of many church and neighborhood groups that have now organized community garden spaces for themselves. This movement has roots in the old Victory Gardens of World War II, and it is an idea that deserves wider consideration.

2. Growing a window garden.

Lettuce works well year-round in a sunny window spot, and if you get a cut-and-come-again variety like Winter Green Jewel romaine, then you can grow it, cut it, and grow it again repeatedly, making very efficient use of a small space.

3. If possible, look up.

This last idea may not be for everyone, but I had an older divorced woman with some health issues come to several of my classes, and she was determined to get healthier and live more frugally because her money situation was very tight. She was living in an apartment with no access at all to garden space, but after one of my classes, she decided to approach her landlord about gardening on a flat part of the roof, and the landlord agreed. Today this friend of mine has been able to move to a more rural county and has access to a full garden she shares with a friend. But she got her start on a roof because of sheer tenacity! Remember, what you focus on expands.

The author's garden behind his rental apartment in 1999. The author only signed a lease after the landlord agreed to let the author turn unused space into a vegetable garden.

If you are an established gardener:

1. Begin winter gardening.

It's the easiest gardening you'll ever do—no pests or bugs, very little watering, very little time required, just lots of fresh eating! My book *Backyard Winter Gardening* has all the details for winter gardening without artificial heat or electricity in any climate. For a list of winter garden seeds, visit SeedRenaissance.com.

2. Go stress-free.

Begin to transition from a labor-intensive garden to a more bountiful garden with less stress and expense by growing the self-seeding vegetables listed in this book and by making use of the wild edible vegetables as explained in this book.

The author on the day he graduated from Brigham Young University, posing for a picture in his garden on land borrowed from an elderly neighbor couple. Today, Caleb Warnock is nearly 50 pounds lighter than his weight in this photo, after years of working to eat more healthily.

3. Live fresh.

Commit to eating something from your property every day as much as possible. Work on having a full meal at least once a week serving nothing but food from your property.

4. Open your mouth.

Talk to your kids (or grandkids) about gardening. Invite them into your garden to both plant and harvest, and share your excess vegetables with your family and neighbors.

In this day and age, some people in your family won't be in the habit of eating vegetables, let alone growing them. I'm convinced this is because they don't know what real food tastes like. Think about it—if the only green beans you had ever tasted came from a grocery store can, would you eat them?

I wouldn't.

On a whim, I tried a can of peaches from the store once. They were horrible. There is no other word to describe them. If that's what I thought peaches tasted like—hard and rubbery with a cloying syrup—I wouldn't eat them. So if you have some of these non-vegetable eaters in your family, don't spend another minute worrying about it. They will come around when the raspberries are in season. Everyone starts somewhere. And if you don't have a peach tree, for heaven's sake, go to your local farmers' market in August. These small steps are how non-vegetable eaters become people who love vegetables, once they've learned what real, fresh, local food tastes like.

NO GOOD, GOOD, BETTER, BEST

While you are thinking about your self-sufficiency, think of the "no good, good, better, best" scale. What is "no good" for your family is to set goals that are unrealistic or forced. If you hate vegetables, growing kohlrabi isn't going to be any use to you (I promise). Coming home from the farmers' market with a fresh rutabaga isn't likely to inspire change (even though rutabaga, when fresh and prepared correctly, is mouthwatering.)

Trying to go from zero to fully self-reliant overnight is going to fail. What you need to decide is how your family can move forward—from where you are to the next step.

Make sure, as you jump into becoming more self-reliant, that you only take steps that you can sustain. I've seen too many families try to do too much or move too fast, only to watch their efforts collapse around them because they could not sustain their enthusiasm or transition to a new lifestyle. If you don't grow a garden, commit to visit your local farmers' market. Ask a friend with a garden if you can buy some carrots from them. Whatever moves your family from where you are to one step better—that is what you need to do.

Work on the metaphorical low-hanging fruit first, and what will make the most dramatic impact to your health and your budget. Eventually, plant a small garden and work toward making a single self-sufficient meal or two. Forget about year-round self-sufficient eating for now, and forget about going all gung ho with a huge garden that you won't have time or energy to sustain. Here are some starting places:

1. Vow to get started on self-reliance but not to get overwhelmed. If you save one dollar on one grocery store trip, then you have started. Next time, save two dollars.

2. Replace a frozen or processed meal—or fast-food restaurant stop—with a quick and easy homemade meal like toast and eggs, an omelet, or a green salad.

3. Choose not to buy or eat any processed foods for a week or a month.

4. Choose to stop drinking soda. Try making punch with powdered stevia extract instead.

5. Ask friends and family for their favorite recipes made mostly of fresh vegetables—then make one.

6. In summer, ask friends and neighbors for any extra garden produce they may have. Promise them you will make sure none of it goes to waste, then keep that promise.

7. Learn to cook with herbs and seasonings. Choose a backyard herb—oregano, for example—and ask around for anyone who has great recipes with oregano. Tell people you are trying to learn to cook with fresh herbs and seasonings, and ask for help and advice.

8. In summer, give the kids (or grandkids) a small backyard space and let them plant some favorite vegetable seeds. Explain to them that they will need to make one family meal, with your help, at harvest time and that they will be in charge of weeding and watering their vegetables (with help and guidance).

9. Serve something at least partially self-sufficient at every holiday meal, and explain to everyone eating which ingredients are self-sufficient and why self-reliance is important to you. Talk about the food you used to eat as a child when you visited your grandparents.

10. For one month, eat only sweets and treats that you make at home from scratch (even if the ingredients are store bought).

11. Examine exactly how much you spent on groceries and eating out over the past month and past three months. Make changes to bring this number down.

12. Start keeping a log of all the wasted food you throw away. What are you throwing away and why? How much are you spending on this wasted food?

ADVANCED SELF-RELIANCE

Most of us will never be 100 percent self-sufficient when it comes to daily meals, but there is much joy and personal pride in being able to say you have achieved a self-reliant milestone. At our house, we "notch off" vegetables one at a time—never having to buy carrots, for example, because we have our own

365 days a year. When it comes to eating, advanced self-reliance is all about being able to say you have accomplished being totally self-sufficient at providing certain key ingredients for family meals.

Below are lists of what our family is able to eat totally and partially self-sufficiently, what we want to be self-sufficient at, and what we recognize we will likely never be able to provide self-sufficiently. This is not a blueprint for your family, but we get asked a lot about what we eat, so I provide this to both satiate people's curiosity and to inspire you to what is possible.

We 98–100 percent self-sufficiently provide

- onions
- carrots
- lettuce and salad greens
- green beans
- eggs
- cabbage
- summer squash
- winter squash
- beef
- jam
- jelly
- leeks
- rutabaga
- beets
- turnips

We 80–90 percent self-sufficiently provide

- potatoes
- tomatoes
- cooking herbs (oregano, thyme, parsley, lemon balm, chives, garlic chives, etc.)
- blackberries

We are partially self-sufficient on, and working to improve,

- backyard fruit juices
- raspberries
- wheat and flour
- peas
- cantaloupe
- medicinal herbs
- tomato sauce

In the winter months, we sparingly buy

- cucumbers
- corn on the cob
- celery
- strawberries
- watermelon
- cantaloupe

We are not even trying to be self-sufficient on

- dairy (milk, cheese, butter, cottage cheese, ice cream)
- bacon (My wife will not let me have a pig. I've begged.)

We buy in bulk for storage

- some wheat
- raw honey
- powdered stevia extract (all-natural herbal sweetener)
- sugar (we have drastically reduced the amount of white sugar we use)
- canned chili
- some tomato sauce
- olives
- refried beans
- taco seasoning
- chicken soup (for days we're all sick in bed)

Things we could be self-sufficient on but aren't because of time constraints:

- ketchup
- mayonnaise
- Dry pasta. I do make fresh pasta, but I never seem to have time to make lots of it to dry for later use.
- flour tortillas
- Chicken. We do harvest and eat our own chickens, but because we sell eggs and hens, and we don't eat that much chicken, we do buy chicken from the store sometimes instead of taking a layer from our flock.

Things we almost never buy (and why):

FROZEN PRE-PACKAGED MEALS

They are expensive and often far less healthy that what we would make at home. I remember once seeing a moment on a television show where a famous rich person asked her chef to make her waffles for breakfast, and her chef went to a huge top-end freezer and pulled out a package of frozen waffles to put in a toaster. How can you call yourself a chef if you are feeding people frozen waffles, especially when you could whip up waffle batter from scratch in the amount of time it would take to toast the frozen ones?

BOXES OF PROCESSED FOODS

They are unnecessary. Pancake mixes, canned soups, breakfast cereals, cake mixes—I'm struggling to even think of what boxed food to list because it's been so long since we've had any.

SNACK FOODS, LIKE POTATO CHIPS

We buy them a couple times a year for indulgent picnics in the canyon. We don't make a habit of it.

BAKERY COOKIES, PIES, OR BARS

They are expensive and hardly ever taste wonderful. I believe that you can eat whatever you want and still be healthy so long as you make it from scratch in your own kitchen.

ANYTHING THAT HAS A COMMERCIAL

Food that requires a commercial is not food—it's corporate nonsense. You don't ever see a commercial for fresh carrots or green beans, for example. But you will see commercials for sugary foods, patented foods, snack foods, and processed foods that are made in factories and full of stuff you shouldn't be eating. There is a long line of companies ready to take your money for their unhealthy products. They don't have

your family's health in mind, and they won't be there to help with the health crisis that eating those foods always leads to.

Bonus list—"foods" avoided by every family that prizes health:

BREAKFAST CEREALS

For two years my wife and I were the nursery teachers for the toddlers in our local church, and I could tell every single week which children had been fed a breakfast of sugar, whether it was cereal or pancakes drowning in sugar syrup. What you feed a child for breakfast has an enormous influence on their behavior. I've also worked hard to get away from buying breakfast cereal because if you can get away from breakfast cereal, you can really start going to the grocery store less often. Pancakes are fast, and my waffles are famous (and fast). Breakfast can be as simple as a fried backyard egg.

JUICE

As I write this, we have just finished a big family dinner at our house. It's only a Thursday evening, but we've had extended family staying with us for ten days, so our supper looked like a Sunday evening meal. Our youngest grandson, fourteen months old, had surgery this morning and is suffering. We are grateful for modern medicine and equally grateful to have this day nearly behind us. For all these reasons, our meal felt special, and when a meal is an occasion at our house, we go into the basement cold room and bring up some of our homemade grape juice, canned from our backyard grapes. We had three quarts tonight. Xander and Conrad, seven and six years old respectively, proudly brought it upstairs for me. We poured it from my favorite pottery jug, hand-thrown by a local artist.

Now, having said all that, let me say this: If you want healthy kids, don't buy them juice. We don't have television at our house anymore, but before we got rid of it, I observed that juice commercials were peppered among the shows for kids. According to the "2012 State of the Industry Report" for beverages, we as a nation spent a staggering 2.7 billion dollars on juice just from the top ten brands in 2012.[1] Juice commercials feature the most adorable children, with adorable voices and mannerism, and the message is always that juice is good for them.

This is a lie being told for money.

Without pulp, juice is digested by the body as though it is refined white sugar, meaning it immediately spikes the glycemic index. This nearly instantly causes the behavior of children to change toward feral, and in the long term it puts them at risk of developing diabetes.

Most of the vitamins found in store-bought juice are totally synthetic—added to the juice as powders at the manufacturing plant, even when the juice is labeled as 100 percent natural. According to federal law, juice can still be labeled as 100 percent natural even when synthetic, factory-created vitamins have been stirred in.

If you give an orange to a child to eat, the natural sugars in the orange do not spike their glycemic index. If you give them the same amount of orange juice that they would have gotten from eating that orange, it does spike their glycemic index. This is because juice without the rest of the fruit is just candy water—it's sugar. It's a dessert. Without the fiber, the sugars rush into the digestive tract. With the fiber, the sugars are digested much more slowly and healthily. Not to mention that chewing fruit fiber helps clean teeth and strengthen gums. Drinking juice encourages cavities.

Tropicana Pure Premium is the best-selling juice brand in the US, according to the beverage industry report.[2] Tropicana Pure Premium is wholly owned by Pepsi. Many juice brands are owned by soda companies. They advertise juice heavily to children (and their parents) as a health drink. What they know—what they don't tell you—is that getting children off of milk and water at daily meals sets a beautiful (to the soda shareholders) pattern of sugar and soda addiction for life. Soda addiction is a demon that is hard for adults to control, let alone children.

Soda companies are spending billions on advertising to set a pattern for your kids. They want your kids to grow up to spend money on a desperate life-long addiction to sugary drinks.

Letting kids develop the habit of drinking water and milk at meals means fewer dental bills, fewer glycemic problems (diabetes) down the road, and a higher chance of making it through the sugar trap later on (the soda companies won't give up, though). In a lot of American homes, the battle is lost—the kids grow up watching their parents drink soda. Those kids are all going to grow up drinking soda and struggling with weight and adult-onset diabetes. Choose to protect your kids by giving them milk and water, not juice.

SODA

Soda has not a single redeeming quality, yet most of America hauls it around, sucking on it like a baby bottle. It ravages teeth. It makes you fat. It wrecks havoc on the glycemic index. Worst of all, it is as bad as smoking when it comes to masking the true flavor of food—no one eating a sugary drink at a meal can taste the natural sugar in a carrot, for example, because the natural sugars in a carrot cannot compete with the industrial sweetness of processed white sugar or high-fructose corn syrup. People who sell sugary foods are not motivated by your health, and when your health is gone, those people will be too, with lots of your money. One day perhaps we can have an honest conversation about sugar in this country. Meanwhile, parents must be having that conversation in their homes because every time we choose soda, we are stepping into a vicious circle of diabetes, obesity, and inflammation—even allergies are exacerbated by sugar.

WHITE FLOUR

White flour is digested by the body exactly as though it is white sugar because all starches are converted to glucose in the digestion process. White flour spikes the glycemic index exactly like white sugar. This is because most of the natural fiber has been stripped away. If you eat whole wheat flour, which leaves the fiber intact, the glycemic index is not spiked because the conversion of starch to sugar is slowed to its natural rate.

White flour is also the primary cause of heartburn, and in my experience, about half of all people who have severe heartburn can get rid of it simply by switching to whole wheat flour. (The other half can get rid of it by switching to whole wheat flour with natural yeast).

Whether it's sugary cereal, juice, soda, or white flour—all things our ancestors did without for their entire lives—the real issue to me is our children and grandchildren.

A couple years ago, I attended a private event at the zoo in our state. The entire zoo was rented out for the evening, closed to the public, by one of the largest employers in our state, which happens to be a medical company.

I hardly saw the animals. What I could not peel my eyes from was the obese children.

How did we come to this?

There were thousands of people at this event. Waiting in line for the carousel is when I realized that every other child there was morbidly obese. Huge, fat children.

Heartbreaking.

This is the parents' fault.

If you have a ten-year-old who has to waddle because he is so obese, you are responsible. I understand this is a sensitive subject, but if you have a fat child, ask yourself these questions:

Do you feed him sugary cereal for breakfast, or do you make him whole wheat, natural yeast pancakes with baked, low-sugar jam instead of syrup?

Does your obese child watch television during daylight hours? Or play outside?

Does your obese child eat out of your backyard garden more often than he eats at a quick-food restaurant?

Morbid obesity is a death sentence. If your children want to grow up and get themselves fat, that is one thing. But if we never gave them health to begin with, then shame on us. We can decide today to change the fate of these children. If we love our country, then we will do whatever is necessary to give us back our next generation.

This chapter is about the future—planning now to accomplish the goals that will increase our future self-reliance. No one in the future will be less self-reliant than those adults who began life as seriously obese children. These future adults will likely be doomed to fight for their health every day of their adult lives. This fight will suck up their energy, their time, and their finances. People who are battling for their very health have little left to give back to the community, whether it be time for family, volunteering, or teaching classes. What we will need most in the future will be people who are healthy—we will need them to fight for our nation, create art, expand science, educate, sacrifice for families, and contribute to society and the greater good of communities and nations. Sick people aren't likely to have that freedom.

Childhood is the time to create possibilities for future adults, not strip them of the foundation of their future health.

Notes

1. "2012 State of the Industry Report," *Beverage Industry*.

2. Ibid.

Reeds and flowers growing in the author's backyard pond.

CHAPTER 4

CHARM IS WASTED ON EARTH AND SKY:

THE CABINET OF CURIOSITIES

To me, this is the most important chapter in this book.

A deep and natural love of science, art, and learning is what defined the Renaissance in Europe beginning in the fourteenth century. After my first Forgotten Skills book came out, several bloggers and even some of my friends started referring to me as "a modern Renaissance man," which—I cannot tell a lie—I loved. I loved it so much, I've adopted the term. My seed company is called SeedRenaissance .com because it is time for us to think in a new way about what we want from our seeds and what kind of seeds we want in the world, as I discussed in my first book.

The actual Renaissance was four hundred years (give or take) of startling advances in human thinking about what was possible and what was meaningful. The period was marked by one of my favorite things in the world, the Cabinet of Curiosities. For middle-income families, this was a simple cabinet; for wealthy families they became entire rooms and halls filled with curiosities from around the world—egg shells, dried botanicals, telescopes and lenses, the

The author's collection of "museum eggs," which are eggs from the author's chickens with unusual colors, patterns, or sizes, as discussed in the first Forgotten Skills book. These eggs are part of the author's personal Cabinet of Curiosities.

A shed skin from one of the author's *Henries*, as the garden snakes are called. These snakes never have teeth, are perfectly harmless, and eat thousands of slugs and bugs in their lifetimes.

sun-dried electric-blue body of a dragonfly, exotic minerals and crystals, empty nests, shed snake skins, and books that teach. Actually, this is just a small list of what is in my own modern-day Cabinet of Curiosities, which now stretches into several rooms of the house. The goal was to excite the human mind to what was possible, to visually prove that there was a lot of cool stuff out there in the world that deserved our time for exploration and study. The intensity of curiosity from the fourteenth to the seventeenth centuries—the sheer excitement for delving into the natural world to see what was really there, how things worked, and how to harness science and art for the common benefit—is hard to fathom today.

Is there any of this noble spirit left?

Instead of cabinets of natural wonders, today's families are much more likely to have "collected" a television set coupled to a game console—just about the two sorriest substitutes I can think of for actual curiosity about the natural world.

It's time again for families to keep cabinets of true natural wonders. Among the greatest needs for the rising generation is a reminder of what money cannot buy—the world that surrounds us, the nature of earth. In a culture defined by electronics, it is up to us to create a backyard renaissance for our kids and grandkids.

SOME SUGGESTIONS FOR STARTING YOUR OWN COLLECTION, AND HOW TO USE IT:

1. Start in your backyard. There are incredible things to be found in our own backyards, if we look. While gardening, I have shoveled up pieces of an antique metal stove and metal farm equipment that is at least a half-century old. I've found old glass marbles and beautiful chunks of minerals and crystals—copper veins, quartz shards, milky quartz pebbles. Nothing terribly valuable, but all of it interesting and worthy of attention, conversation, and showing around the family. And then there are the blue shells of robin eggs—the grandkids and I found one while weeding the tomatoes, and they were so excited when I let them hold it and explained to them that the baby bird that once lived in the shell was now flying in the trees. We carefully gathered the delicate shell halves to add to our collection. Every year we have blue dragonflies that make our backyard pond their home, and every fall we find their beautiful dead exoskeletons, complete with delicate wings. There are skins and skeletons of garden snakes—we found another one last week at the time of this writing. Xander has been able to identify the footprints of deer in our garden since he was three years old—along with the footprints of

our chickens, dogs, and cat. He sometimes carefully scoops them out of the mud to dry for his collections (which are not as carefully curated as mine, so to speak, so if we really want to keep something, he lends it to my collection.) There are empty bird nests, huge bubbles of dried yellow resin from our pine trees, curious insects, beetles, and moths that we sometimes have to look up. There are dried reeds from the pond, and tiny fossils embedded in rocks, waiting to be found for who knows how many years. There are dried coneflowers that stand outside as statues in the snow in winter. There are endless things to see, taste, smell, touch, feel, and collect for your own Cabinet of Curiosities.

2. Observe the natural world. One of my grandpa Robert Warnock's most startling gifts in life was his ability to see things that no one else noticed—a skill which aided him well in his profession as a chemist. On countless occasions he took me and my cousins on walks—along highways and dirt paths, through forests and deserts and mountain trails. He loved to hunt for fossils, gems, minerals, interesting rocks, unusual natural objects of any kind. There was not a corner of the earth he was not intensely interested in. I loved to go on these walks with him because he could find treasures. Literally. We would be walking through the family farm and he would bend down, brush at the dirt, and pull out an ancient arrowhead. Or a topaz crystal, a fossilized leaf, a chunk of quartz, or a pebble of sandstone that had been dripped on for so long a hole had formed in its center. He would get change at the grocery store and pull out a World War II wheat penny, or a silver dime or quarter. He knew his stuff, and he had a keen eye. He also had extraordinary respect for nature, so let me say this: Take only what belongs to you, or what you have permission to remove. Don't take anything from national park land (which is illegal) and don't take anything from private land without permission. Be aware and be fair.

3. Collect objects without price. As you can see from the above examples, a Cabinet of Curiosities is not something that should cost money, with very few exceptions. The goal is not to buy your way to a collection. The goal is to get yourself and your family out into the natural world and bring back some special pieces. For example, we have a friend who has collected heart-shaped rocks for decades on her walks and journeys. Our family likes to spend time, when possible, on the coast of Oregon. There are shops full of expensive seashells there—most of them not naturally found in Oregon and marked with a China import sticker. There are beautiful and interesting—and pricey—shells in those shops, and with a credit card you could buy your way to quite a collection. But that would defeat the purpose of a Cabinet of Curiosities. Instead, you have to walk the shoreline to find the sand dollars and

A page from the author's college botany notebook of dried plants.

the sun-bleached bits of coral and choose a couple to take home. If you are lucky, and observant, you might find some water-polished sea glass or a shark tooth. The personal meaning of a shell you buy at a shop will be fleeting, but the shell you collect from the spot where the ocean meets the edge of the earth will be a memory forever, growing in fondness and good feelings more as each year passes and the children grow up. Curiosities are for finding, not buying.

That said, there are perhaps a few exceptions. My reward for myself after we paid off our house was to purchase a large telescope, something I had been hoping to afford for years. With a bit more breathing room in our finances, I was able to save up four hundred dollars, and the telescope will last the rest of my life, with care. My grandpa Warnock also had a telescope on a wooden stand, and he took us out to observe the heavens on countless nights. Everything I know about astronomy I learned from him, and it was important to me to buy a good and useful piece of equipment, not something expensive. I have also purchased a couple of small magnifying lenses, and we are saving up for a microscope that will take pictures—the big kids (my stepdaughters) have become so impatient with my "saving" that they offered to go in on it with me, and I'll probably take them up on the offer. Can I tell you the joy it brings me that they are so excited to get a microscope? Of course, the only reason we buy these items is because they are not something we could make at home, at least not sufficiently to accomplish our goals. But they are useful tools for observing the natural world up close.

4. "Collect" the uncollectible. Many wonders of nature can't be kept in a cabinet—and you have to spend time outside to even observe them. I love to point out blue bees, which are so important in the garden, but hardly anyone has ever heard of them, let alone seen them—and yet they are around us all summer. And solitary bees, praying mantises, huge earthworms in the compost pile, hummingbirds flitting among the butterfly bushes, voles hiding under a log, water skeeters on the backyard pond, goldfish eating insect larvae, bees drinking water, snow being pulled from the top of Mount Timpanogos by a high invisible wind on a bright winter day, the Pleiades and Orion in the winter sky, moss growing on the north face of the barn in winter, the tip of an apple tree branch captured in an icicle, a soaring hawk or vulture (run, chickens, run!), the smell of the antique rose bushes, and the perfume of grape hyacinths—all of these things are fleeting and filled with joy. They remind me of the 1847 poem by Ralph Waldo Emerson that I love:

THE RHODORA

On being asked, whence is the flower.

In May, when sea-winds pierced our solitudes,
I found the fresh Rhodora in the woods,
Spreading its leafless blooms in a damp nook,
To please the desert and the sluggish brook.
The purple petals fallen in the pool
Made the black water with their beauty gay;
Here might the red-bird come his plumes to cool,
And court the flower that cheapens his array.
Rhodora! if the sages ask thee why
This charm is wasted on the earth and sky,
Tell them, dear, that, if eyes were made for seeing,
Then beauty is its own excuse for Being;
Why thou wert there, O rival of the rose!
I never thought to ask; I never knew;
But in my simple ignorance suppose
The self-same power that brought me there,
   brought you.[1]

5. House a special collection. Children and grand-children take cues from us while figuring out what in the world around them is important and worthy. If you spend most of your evenings watching television, they will observe that this is your priority, and their observation will likely influence them for life. If you spend your evenings taking walks and talking to them, they will observe that they are important to you. One way to show children that the natural curiosities in your "cabinet" are special is to give them special housing. I'm not suggesting that you spend a bunch of money—one of the most special pieces of furniture in our family is the small cabinet that my great-grandfather made for one of his collections. If you have the ability to make a special cabinet, you should. I don't, but I buy interesting inexpensive boxes and unique sets of drawers whenever I find them. I have a roll-top desk with all kinds of little trinkets tucked inside, and I have a set of drawers purchased from a local craftsman carved from a stump of worm-carved cedar. It speaks to my soul (which is why I got it as a gift, after broad hints, for Father's Day.) You can dedicate a high shelf or part of a china cabinet. Your cabinet doesn't have to be expensive, but it should be obvious to all that what is in it is treasured and important and worthy of special care and attention. The way you treat your collection and speak of it will make it special to the young people you are hoping to influence—and those moments with you, when you let them hold a piece of your collection, will be memories that will last forever and instruct a lifelong love of learning.

I cannot end this chapter without saying a word about investing in play.

Xander is our oldest grandchild, and when he was young, I was one of his primary caretakers. In his second year, I let him start watching some very

The author's grandchildren are allowed and encouraged to play in the backyard pond, which was designed to be only 6 inches deep for safety.

The author's backyard sandbox is part of his investment in the grandkids and is the most popular backyard feature—used even more than the zip line.

old children's videos we had in the house, and then we decided to get television, and we would occasionally let him watch some kids' shows. Fairly quickly, he went from being a boy who could not wait to go outside to play to being a child who begged and then demanded to watch movies and television. This started to drive me crazy, so I began to severely limit the amount of television time he could have, justifying even that by telling myself that it was really for me—if he'd sit and watch a movie, I could get important work done. Then came the day that we were driving somewhere, and Xander saw a McDonald's restaurant out the window—a place where he had never been, to my knowledge. Not only did he know the name of the restaurant on sight, but he also knew they had a play area and a toy inside the kid's

meal. I was gobsmacked. "Where did you hear about McDonald's and the toys?" I asked him with an even voice. And he named one of the supposedly educational children's shows he was allowed to watch on our new cable subscription.

To make matters worse, a day or two later, he asked me for a very expensive plastic toy and quoted what was obviously an advertisement line about the toy. Where had he heard of this toy? Again he named a television program. That was the day that the rules at our house changed. From that day on, the videos and the television were gone. For a day or two Xander was petulant, but then he went back outside to play.

Was it harder on me? Yes. I remember clearly the day I was doing a phone interview with longtime US

Senator Orrin Hatch, and Xander got on the other line and started talking and would not get off. There were innumerable times when it would have been more convenient to park him in front of a television. But I wasn't willing to let the television continue to distort his values and take advantage of his impressionable mind. The difference in his attitude and language was undeniable.

Slowly I began to realize that money invested in the backyard—or art supplies—is never wasted. We built a little sandbox. As the number of grandkids increased, the popularity of the sandbox did not decrease, so we made it bigger—and then bigger. I'm pretty sure it is now the world's largest backyard sandbox. It's the square footage of a condo I once owned, almost literally. The grandkids have spent at least thousands of hours in it collectively. It's the most popular thing in our yard. I have purchased a collection of kid-sized shovels, not cheap plastic ones but real metal and wood, which took quite some time to find. The kids use these to work in the garden, and they love them. I bought them their own kid-sized garden gloves. I put a swing in the maple tree. I bought a one-hundred-dollar metal swing set and slide at Walmart, which has lasted six years now in great condition. When he was four, Xander and I built a clubhouse. Last week, he and his cousin and my wife repainted it—they had a blast. Last year, I spent two hundred dollars to install a backyard zip line because the kids are getting older. This month we had to take it down and hoist it a few feet higher because the two oldest grandkids were dragging on the ground, they have gotten so big. A decade ago, we built a backyard pond from scratch, twenty-five feet by twenty-five feet, using a few dollars' worth of cheap 6-mil painters plastic (six layers) as the lining and stocked it with ten-cent goldfish, which grew to be six inches long. We don't ever have to feed them because they eat larvae, moss, and bugs and they overwinter under the ice, and the dogs love to play in the pond on hot summer days just as much as the kids do. (Except for one wintering hole for the fish, we keep it six inches deep so there are no worries of accidental drowning.) They all love to toss pebbles and skip stones in the pond. This summer at the time of this writing, Xander has been ferreting crystals from the rocks in the driveway and selling them for pennies to the neighbors, going door to door!

For the winter months, we buy washable paint and dollar-store colored paper, glue sticks, wooden craft sticks, and all kinds of inexpensive art supplies for the kids to do. They all do origami—animals and towers, cups and boxes—and they all love to fold and race paper airplanes. They draw in notebooks and have written hundreds of kid-sized letters and notes. (One day, after Xander got into trouble for a bad decision, he wrote me a full-page letter that was so touching I framed it. It made me cry.) We have memberships at three or four excellent nearby museums. We make homemade play dough and volcanoes with baking soda and vinegar in big kitchen bowls (I learned the bowl part the hard way). We make low-sugar cookies, and the kids are all learning to cook as appropriate for their age level. Xander at age seven now cooks several simple dishes by himself without supervision because he's been cooking for years. I bought hand drills from an antique store for them to use for woodworking (much safer than electric drills) and fishing supplies and real tools for their own little toolboxes. (Another hard-learned lesson: Expect hours of hands-and-knees cleanup if you let a child take a box of nails to the back lawn.) All six grandkids are allowed to take pictures with my expensive camera (after a talk with me), which I use to take photos for my books. I'll also mention that it's not all play—they all help clean the house. As I write this, we just had all six grandkids here with us for three weeks in June, and every single day, they played and worked until they fell into bed at night—the best sign of a successful day.

There are probably hundreds of kids books—at our house, if you've had a bad day, or a good day, or done a good job, or made a good decision, you get to go to Grandpa's Book Box and pick out a brand-new children's book to keep. There is no soda here, and if you want cookies, they have to be made from scratch with the kids' help. We do countless science projects—Xander leads the way in these. We build together, weed together, plant the garden and harvest together, and play and lie in the hammock together and look at the stars. (I won't lie, the children have also invented the game of tumbling each other out of the hammock. They do it for hours.)

I mention all this to demonstrate that my wife and I have made a decision to invest in play. Really, this is a decision to invest in their health—body, brain, and soul. There will be no obese, television-guzzling couch-children at our house. There will be no McDonald's-indoctrinating commercials. Nothing—no amount of Cabinets of Curiosities nor money spent on books or "educational" movies nor passes to museums—surpasses the importance of simply letting children invent their own play and explore the natural world, both outside and inside the house. Personalities are forged in the dirt and paint. Memories are built. Cousins become lifelong best friends—I can vouch from experience. Creativity becomes natural, and so does physical fitness. (My

grandpa let the grandkids race-climb his flagpole. The last time we all gathered to watch this was on the day of his and Grandma's joint funeral. They were there watching.) Most important, a love of life and learning is born. These are the traits and experiences that turn children into useful adults. Children are the most fascinating and valuable natural wonder the world has ever produced. They deserve our best energy and thinking.

Our lives are not perfect and the kids and grand-kids aren't perfect either. But my wife and I will spend our last breath working to be the best influence on them we know how to be. We try to discern what kind of world they will face when they are parents themselves, and what kinds of skills and talents they will need to learn from us. Every man and woman faces tests of courage and morality. We want them to grow up to be self-reliant, strong, worthy, and useful to their communities and nation. We make our expectations clear, both in writing (we have framed rules on the kitchen wall) and in conversation.

Last, I'll repeat a piece of advice given to me by my great-aunt that has changed my life. When a child is misbehaving or out of control, the best medicine is to quietly sit them on your lap and hug them, and hug them, and hug them, and then listen while they tell you their feelings.

Notes

1. Emerson, "The Rhodora."

CHAPTER 5
LIQUID OF LIFE:
COLLECTING WATER FROM RAIN AND SNOW

A friend of mine who runs a preparedness website recently passed around a design for collecting water from the roof. The first moment I saw the plan, I could tell it was just theory—untested and not based on anyone's real-life experience.

Anyone who followed the design would be in for heartburn.

I've learned the hard way that a water collection system must work in the dead of winter while withstanding terrible winds and storms, summer dust and sandstorms, pasture animals, and children. I live in the Utah desert—we get snow in winter, and some rain in fall and spring. Summer does not provide enough rain to keep anything alive. The collection system my friend was passing around involved taking two large plastic garbage cans and cutting a hole into the lid so a gutter could drain right into the can. The two cans were supposed to sit on a specially made heavy wooden table. You were supposed to cut holes in the bottoms of the plastic cans to install several pipes, fittings, and taps so you could turn the water on and off at will. The whole plan would work like a charm in a charmed world where there is great

weather, no winter, and no wind. That is not the world I garden in.

It would never work on our property. Knowing why is instructive.

If the plastic garbage pails were ever empty of water, the wind where we live would quickly blow them to the next county. If they were full of water, the wind would blow the lids to the Land of Oz. When the collected water would freeze inside in winter, the cheap plastic would split and be ruined. The holes in the lid for the gutter would drown our curious chickens—and possibly raccoons and other thirsty intruders, spoiling the water in the process. Not to mention that our winds would blow dust, dirt, leaves, and seeds into the water barrel constantly. The tap pipes and fittings at the base would plug right up. The bad design my friend was passing around was cheap—a weekend project. The plan was from an emergency preparedness book. The author said it was a great system for water storage, domestic supply, firefighting, and emergency use. But I didn't think it was a system anyone had ever actually tried to use in a real situation. My work to collect rain and

This simple gutter system collects rain and snowmelt from the roof of the author's barn, funneling the water into a barrel inside the barn.

The author between two water collection barrels inside his greenhouse.

snow water was born of necessity. When I designed my geothermal greenhouse, I knew it needed to be completely self-sustaining—there would be no electricity, no artificial heating or cooling—just walls, a roof, sun, and earth. Running water was not possible. (You can read about my greenhouse, designed to grow food 365 days a year, in my book *Backyard Winter Gardening*.) There was a frost-free water line near the location, but it had been broken and turned off for years, and repairing it was prohibitively expensive. (We have since had it fixed. It cost more than six hundred dollars, money that we did not have at the time.) The only way to have water through the winter in the greenhouse was to haul it a long distance by buckets despite the weather and temperature.

Or we could collect water from the roof.

To be honest, designing the roof collection system was much harder than I had imagined. There was no reference for building a geothermal greenhouse—I had not been able to find anyone in the United States with anything like what I was trying to design. Creating a design for the greenhouse took so many hours of research and planning and consulting with my contractor that when it was completed in February, I had a brand-new greenhouse with no water. I put a gutter on the bottom of the slanting roof and considered drilling holes into the timber walls to allow the water to follow gravity into the greenhouse—but so much effort, planning, and expense had been spent to make the polycarbonate roof and walls strong and insulated that I was afraid drilling through would compromise the whole thing. After all, even a tiny air leak on a twenty-below-zero night could kill a greenhouse, which is heated only by the natural heat of the earth in winter. I talked to plumbers and more experts and eventually drilled and installed a custom fitting into the gutter, allowing me to attach a regular garden hose. The hose used gravity to take the water from the roof, snaking around to the back of the greenhouse where the hose could enter at ground level, avoiding the polycarbonate walls facing the southern sun.

The system worked—for a while. Heavy winter snow often overwhelmed the gutter, but all I needed was enough water to fill two fifty-five-gallon barrels inside the greenhouse, and I got what I needed. By the time that first winter was over, heavy snow and ice had begun to damage the gutter, causing it to sag and distend. In the spring, our cows and horse eventually damaged the gutter beyond repair. I needed a fence around the greenhouse to keep the animals away and replace the entire gutter and capture system—and I wanted to capture more water. I'd gotten by with enough water, but only because on the coldest days, when the drain hose was frozen, I scooped snow into buckets to let the sun melt it in the greenhouse.

The greenhouse was built as an extension of our pasture barn solely so we could avoid having to get a building permit from the city (in our city, extending an existing barn required no new permit). I wanted to collect water from the roof of the barn behind the greenhouse—but I couldn't figure out how to get the water to drain into the greenhouse without blocking my access to the only door to the greenhouse. Eventually, I hit on the ideal solution—a removable section of gutter. I installed a gutter on the barn, with a downspout leading directly into the barn, emptying into a fifty-five-gallon barrel just feet from the greenhouse door. The barrel is just a capture tank, but I positioned it so that the southern winter sun falls directly on it. Between storms, the sun gathers enough strength to begin to melt the water in the barrel. I stick a ten-dollar plastic hand pump into the barrel just as soon as enough ice has melted inside the barrel so I can get the pump in. Then I open the door to the greenhouse, position a long piece of gutter from the capture barrel to a storage barrel inside the greenhouse, and allow gravity to drain the water. This system is 100 percent reliable all year round. As I write this, it is July and we had a rare summer rain burst last night—the first rain here in many weeks. I didn't have to run outside or do anything to capture the water—the capture tank is ready for duty whenever water appears from the sky.

RELIABLE AND RELEVANT DESIGN MUST BE PERSONAL

How you design your system will clearly depend on what you are trying to accomplish, and the lay of your land. Some of you reading this might be a bit miffed that I'm not providing you with a choice of layouts and diagrams with measurements and lists of parts and supplies to purchase. There are plenty of books and websites out there with such things, but if you ask me, they are worthless. There is no "one size fits all" water capture system. For your system to be a useful workhorse, you are going to have to design it for your own situation. Here are some hard-learned tips to take into consideration before you get started designing a system:

1. Design for Extremes.

Don't do what I did and waste hundreds of dollars and lots of time and work by trying to build cheap and fast. Instead, follow a modified version of that old woodworking adage, "Measure twice and cut once." For water, the adage would be, "Design twice and build once." First, design your system to meet your needs. Then go back to your design a second time and try to imagine every possible thing that could go wrong. Will it survive a ninety-miles-per-hour windstorm? Curious children? Curious neighborhood children? Livestock? Wild animals? Windblown dirt and sand? Extreme heat? Extreme cold? Before you buy your supplies and build, make sure what you spend your money and time on will last. Otherwise, you will be like me—forced to do the whole thing again.

2. Design for Life.

I once found a garden snake helplessly balanced at the opening in my capture barrel. The creature was so far in it couldn't get out, but it had gotten far enough to realize that if it went any farther, it would fall in and drown. Luckily, I found it when it was still alive and could rescue it. When creating a water capture system, you could be creating a death trap if you are not careful. If there is any possible way that a child of your own, a grandchild, or a neighborhood child could get inside and drown—any possible way at all—then stop and redesign. Above all else, don't create something that could kill a child.

Your design must also consider your homestead population. If you are capturing water for homesteading, chances are you have chickens and perhaps rabbits, goats, and even cows and horses. Can any of the animals get to the system? Could they drown in the system? Could baby animals (like precocious baby chicks) drown in the system? Even if you don't have animals or baby animals now, are you interested in having them in the future? If animals are in your future, design for them now. And remember, chances are that if an animal could drown in your system, a child could too.

Wildlife is also a concern. Raccoons are explorers. Magpies have no fear. Consider squirrels, chipmunks, mice—you don't want a dead mouse in your water tank—voles, gophers, snakes, grasshoppers. Anything that can get in and drown probably will. My fifty-five-gallon barrels have two-inch-diameter holes. I keep the lids closed when not in use. For the capture tank, my downspout goes directly into a funnel, which leaves a space less than the size of a quarter, which so far has been okay to be left open to the elements and animals. Be aware and be careful.

All that said, don't be too concerned about water clarity or dirt, especially if your capture system is just for watering the garden and livestock. Most of the time my water is crystal clear, but if I get to the bottom of a barrel, there is dirt and sand and tree seeds. But all of those things are naturally out in the garden too. I don't put chlorine in my water, but this water is not for human consumption.

3. How Much Water Is Enough?

As you read above, when I first designed my collection system, I was barely able to capture enough water to make it through the first winter, and even that had to be supplemented by gathering snow to melt in the sunny greenhouse. I didn't come anywhere close at that time to having enough water for the greenhouse in summer. I do now. My new system still leaks more water than it captures because I did not level one end of the barn roof gutter correctly,

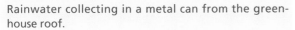

Rainwater collecting in a metal can from the greenhouse roof.

A look at the water collection barrel inside the author's geothermal greenhouse.

so there is still more repair work to do, but I've been lazy about it because the system is capturing enough water for my needs. However, we are not using our system to water our garden right now, and if we ever needed to do that, I would have to fix the gutter that drops water to the ground instead of channeling it to my barrel—and we'd probably have to start collecting water from the house roof too. When you design your capture system, consider your needs now and how those needs might increase in the future. Designing to over-capture is better than designing too small— after all, if you over-capture rainwater and snowmelt, it simply goes into the ground, no harm done.

4. Positioning Your Capture Barrel

I recommend putting your capture tank on firm

ground, not on any kind of a platform. You will read more about this in a moment. I strongly recommend that your capture barrel be as close as possible to where you are going to ultimately use the water, not where you are going to collect the water. This may mean using many feet of gutter or pipe to take the water from the roof where you collect it to the barrel placed where you need the water. If you are really going to use this water, in the long run you will be much happier to have gravity deliver the water to where it is needed instead of you carrying it. Plan wisely.

5. Getting Water In

The longer the gutter that captures your water from the roof, the harder it is to get it level—and if

A specially designed slanting roof on the chicken coop provides water for the horse in winter. An electric trough warmer keeps the water from freezing.

it is not level, water will pool in the gutter and the weight will cause sagging and distension. If you are like me, and you live in a place with snow, you have to be very careful how you position the gutter—if you stick it too far out from the roofline, it will capture all the snow trying to melt off your roof, and collapse under the weight. I have a whole new respect for people who design and install gutter systems after building my collection system on my barn—it's harder than it looks. The gutter needs to stick out under the roofline just enough to capture dripping water, but not so far out that it catches sliding snow. If you are not sure, jury-rig a small section and test it in both rain and snow before you go to the time and expense of installing a whole system, only to discover it doesn't work.

6. Getting Water Out

Most designs recommend elevating your capture tank a couple of feet. This is to make it easier to use gravity to drain your tank. Problem is, creating a platform that will hold the weight of the water safely for years is difficult, expensive, and, if you ask me, a waste of time. The most reliable way of getting water out of your barrel is with a cheap plastic hand pump, which you can buy wherever water storage barrels are sold. Mine cost ten bucks, and it holds up to heat and freezing. The good news is that getting water out of your barrel is no work at all if you follow two guidelines.

1. Keep your barrel more than half full.
2. Keep the watering can or bucket you want to fill on the ground.

If you do these two things, gravity will drain your water for you. All you have to do is get it started. Start the hand pump by pumping the top up and down with your hand a couple times and then gravity takes over and you can just watch the water fill your watering can. Keep your eye on that can or bucket because once it's full, gravity will just keep filling it if you don't take the pump hose out. To fully shut off the flow of water, you will need to lift the pump entirely out of the barrel enough to drain the pump. Or you can leave the pump in the barrel and just make sure the end of the pump hose stays higher than the barrel—then all you have to do next time is put the pump hose in your bucket and it will automatically start without any pumping, so long as your barrel is more than half full of water. After you practice a couple of times, using the hand pump is simple and easy—not to mention inexpensive and reliable.

7. Water for Human Consumption

If you store water for emergency consumption, many places recommend putting bleach into the sealed water barrel. The standard recommendation of the Centers for Disease Control and Prevention is to bring questionable water to a rolling boil for one minute before drinking. Or:

> If you don't have safe bottled water and if boiling is not possible, you often can make water safer to drink by using a disinfectant such as unscented household chlorine bleach or iodine. These can kill most harmful organisms, such as viruses and bacteria, but are not as effective in controlling more resistant organisms such as the parasites Cryptosporidium and Giardia.

To disinfect water,

- Filter it through a clean cloth, paper towel, or coffee filter OR allow it to settle.
- Draw off the clear water.
- To use bleach, add ⅛ teaspoon (or 8 drops; about 0.625 milliliters) of unscented liquid household chlorine (5–6%) bleach for each gallon of clear water (or 2 drops of bleach for each liter or each quart of water),
  - Stir the mixture well.
  - Let it stand for 30 minutes or longer before you use it.
  - Store the disinfected water in clean sanitized containers with tight covers.
- To use iodine, follow the manufacturer's instructions.

Chlorine dioxide tablets are another disinfectant that now is available in some outdoor stores. This disinfectant has proven to be effective against pathogens, including Cryptosporidium, if the manufacturer's instructions are followed.[1]

To sanitize a water storage container, the CDC recommends this:

1. Wash the storage container with dishwashing soap and water and rinse completely with clean water.

2. Sanitize the container by adding a solution made by mixing 1 teaspoon of unscented liquid household chlorine bleach in 1 quart of water.

3. Cover the container and shake it well so that the sanitizing bleach solution touches all inside surfaces of the container.

4. Wait at least 30 seconds and then pour the sanitizing solution out of the container.

5. Let the empty sanitized container air-dry before use OR rinse the empty container with clean, safe water that already is available.[2]

You can read more at www.cdc.gov /healthywater/emergency/safe_water /personal.html.

THE LAWS ARE ALL WET

Whether or not my capture system is legal is a source of debate. For all of modern history, it has been illegal to capture and store any water in my desert state. All natural water belongs to the state and must be allowed to flow freely into the ground along its path to fill the aquifers, lakes, and rivers—predictably, the water rights to those aquifers, lakes, and rivers are astonishingly complex. Suing over water rights is perhaps the most common and popular non-familial legal action in my state. But as homesteading and preparedness have become more important to everyday people, more and more people have begun to install water capture and storage systems—only to discover they are breaking the law. At one point a few years ago, there got to be such an outrage that the state legislature got involved, and a compromise was eventually voted into law. At this writing, the law states that a homeowner must register with the Utah Division of Water Rights (I'm not making this up) "to collect, store, and place the captured precipitation to a beneficial use. . . . A person may collect and store precipitation without registering in no more than two covered storage containers if neither covered container has a maximum storage capacity of greater than 100 gallons."[3]

Oh, and that is not all: "The total allowed storage capacity *with registration* [emphasis added] is no more than 2,500 gallons. Collection and use are limited to the same parcel of land on which the water is captured and stored."[4]

A chicken walks by the underground greenhouse in winter. Note the hose, which collects snowmelt, which gravity feeds into the greenhouse.

When you register with the state, you are issued—again, I am not joking—a "Rainwater Harvesting Registration certificate, which you should print for your records."[5]

I believe in working within the law. I also do not believe in registering my activities with the government if I can possibly avoid it. (My state is now asking people to "voluntarily" register their gardens too, and provide details of what we all grow. We are also supposed to register our chickens.) To stay legal and unregistered, my water collection is limited to two fifty-five-gallon barrels in my greenhouse. I may or may not have a third illegal barrel in my garden (ahem). I don't worry too much about any of it because my storage is not long-term. My water is used to water the greenhouse and garden and, in the winter, the chickens. All of my capturing is fairly temporary because my water is for use, not display. On any given day, the total amount of water I have stored is likely to be less than one hundred gallons total.

Your legal issues will vary depending on where you live. Good luck.

SPEAKING OF CHICKENS

You can use your capture system to water your homestead animals too. To water our cows and horse, I just put the roof collection spout directly into a large trough. It needs to be large so that when it does rain (or the snow melts) there is enough capacity to store all the water you get, which you will need through the dry times. Directing Mother Nature's free water directly into the trough makes it so you don't have to worry about hauling water—let gravity and nature do all the work. At first, I was taking water from the horse trough in a bucket to fill the chicken waterer. Then I realized that if I built a chicken ladder, the chickens could water themselves out of the horse trough. I did have to keep most of the trough covered with plywood so the chickens didn't get in and drown, or get on top and poop in the water. I had to put a little fence around all but one end of the trough to keep the horse from bothering the cover. But once it was all in place, it worked like a charm, and I didn't have to do any work at all. Mother Nature watered all the animals all winter—which was great because at that time my only other option was to haul water in buckets from the house. And horses and cows drink a lot of water.

Whatever you do, make absolutely sure your animals don't run out of water. And remember that livestock—including chickens—eat snow in the winter and melt it in their throats for water. For more details, see my first Forgotten Skills book.

Notes

1. Centers for Disease Control and Prevention, "Personal Preparation and Storage of Safe Water."

2. Ibid.

3. Utah Division of Water Rights, "Rainwater Harvesting Registration."

4. Ibid.

5. Ibid.

The end of a rainbow in the mountains near the author's home.

CHAPTER 6

THE RENAISSANCE OF BARTER, TRADE, AND DICKERING

Recently the technician I hired to set up online sales of my seeds at SeedRenaissance.com sent me a bill for more than six hundred dollars. The amount was more than I had been expecting, so I wrote a quick email to her:

"Thank you, Katie. You do great work. The invoice was a bit painful for me. I have paid you $200 before, and I was hoping this bill would be in the $300 range, for a total of $500. Could we negotiate this bill down a bit?"

Almost immediately, she sent a reply removing one hundred dollars from the bill and offering to remove another one hundred in trade for attendance at one of my eighty-nine-dollar Forgotten Skills classes. I was very happy with this trade and accepted.

Bartering, trading, respectful dickering over prices, and selling handicrafts or niche services on the side—these are forgotten skills experiencing a renaissance in the United States because of the economy. My great-great-great-grandmother sold braided rugs made out of fabric scraps and baskets woven from willows to help keep her family financially solvent in hard times. If she were alive today, she'd be

selling those things on Etsy.com, the famous website that has become the global marketplace for people making handicrafts. For my day job as a journalist, I have interviewed many people using Etsy to at least bring in a healthy dose of extra cash. Some of them are making a nice living and have been doing it for years.

But these days, not everything must be a cash transaction. I recently spoke to an artist who was trading custom portraits for anything she found interesting—for instance, she had traded for a ring. When I asked her why she had turned to bartering, she observed that money is tight for many people, but almost everyone has useful, valuable stuff sitting around their house that they are not using. Why not trade for stuff you need or want?

That philosophy is catching on, and I'm a big supporter.

A couple of weeks ago, my stepdaughter was selling homemade lotion bars at a farmers' market, and a woman offered to trade her twenty-five pounds of raw beeswax for ten lotion bars, which sell for twenty-five dollars for the set. My stepdaughter didn't need the wax because she already had some, but she knew my wife and I would want it, so she accepted the trade, and then had us pay her twenty-five dollars for the wax, which was quite a bit cheaper than what we had been paying for beeswax to make lotions and salves. A successful three-way trade.

One of my most successful three-way trades happened after I started seeing people offering to give away chickens on Freecycle.org. Backyard henkeeping is a growing trend, and these families had enjoyed their first chickens all summer. Now, with winter arriving, the laying was slowing down and the families didn't want to buy feed for them all winter. As I explained in my first book, we don't pay for chicken feed, so I grabbed all the free chickens I could get that autumn—more than twenty hens from six different families. I fed them all winter and collected the eggs. And then, in early summer, I sold seventeen of those laying hens to two different families for a total of 110 dollars. And I could have sold many, many more if I'd had them to sell—we had four other families that wanted to buy hens. The whole endeavor cost me nothing, not even time because I had to feed our chickens anyway. I intend to do the whole thing again this fall. We usually make money by selling eggs from our hens, but selling the free hens was easier than washing eggs and arranging for the buyer to pick them up.

A fan of my books wanted to give copies as gifts. She is from Hawaii and propagates beautiful houseplants from her native state as a hobby. She asked if she could trade a white ginger plant and a plumeria flower plant for a couple books. "If you will deliver the plants to my house," was my response. She immediately agreed. I have traded my books for books from other authors. I have traded my backyard garden seeds for seeds I needed.

A friend who is a radio talk show host was at my home once and was interested in some rare tomato seeds I had purchased. Thinking I could easily get more from my source, I gave them all to her as a gift, to thank her for letting me be on her radio show several times. Later, when it was time to plant the seeds in my geothermal greenhouse in February, those seeds could not be had anywhere on the planet for love nor money. I had totally forgotten that I had given this person seeds two years before. It just so happened that my friend sent me an email saying she had been cleaning and found the seed packet and wondered if they were still good. Not only were they good, I wrote back, but I would like to buy them, please! She immediately wrote back that I could have them for free, and her husband would even deliver them to my door later in the week, even though they lived two counties away. When he arrived, he asked if I would give them a copy of my latest book for delivering the seeds. Definitely! As the scriptures say, ask and ye shall receive!

Then there is horse trading. At one point, my father had a herd of horses on the farm that, it seemed to me, were multiplying like feral cats. My father traded one of those horses for a plane ticket, and another horse for a used car. Pretty savvy.

I once gave away sixty copies of my first Forgotten Skills book at a special event in exchange for an on-your-honor promise from each recipient that they would make a donation to an education charity I wanted to support.

Probably the happiest traders I have ever worked with are my own grandkids. In exchange for their doing some serious and real work in the garden (like filling five-gallon buckets with pebbles when I'm trying to clear new garden space in the pasture), I take the kids to Walmart and let them pick out a ten-dollar

A rustic bench at the foot of the Wasatch Mountains near the author's home.

toy. They even learn negotiating skills along the way. They always pick out (this is no joke—who knew toys were so expensive?) a forty-five-dollar toy first, and then I have to explain the budget to them, and then they dicker (children are natural dickerers) and we settle on a fifteen-dollar toy for each of them. I'm happy that I didn't have to stoop over picking up all those rocks, the work in the garden got done, and they not only got a toy but learned to negotiate too.

I noticed that bartering was gaining national popularity a couple of years ago when I started seeing more and more barter offers appearing randomly on Facebook. Regional barter co-op groups are now popping up on Facebook. The economy is unsteady at best, and the barter system is back. Facebook is also increasingly being used to give things away for free, like leftover yard sale items or extra garden produce or outgrown children's clothes.

If you are new to bartering, here are a few ways to get started:

First off, there is Craigslist, which everyone seems to be using. Craigslist.org has a section for bartering where you can offer your stuff or services for things you need. You can also request services. Even if you don't particularly need anything immediately, it's just plain fun to log on and see what kind of stuff people are bartering. I have noticed that there are a lot of people looking to barter in exchange for dental work, which is a great way for someone without dental insurance to get the healthcare they need without breaking the bank.

Here are some real examples of trades I found offered on Craigslist. I thought they were pretty fascinating:

- "Roofing for dentures. 30-years-experienced

roofer will trade service for dentures for my wife and myself."

• "Local dentist looking to barter dental work generously for the following trades or contractors: vinyl fencing, fence, skilled experienced stucco repair, finish carpentry and cabinets, concrete flatwork, masonry."

• "Local tree company (licensed and insured) will trade our mulch, wood chips and heavies (tree trunks for firewood) in exchange for parking some equipment on your land."

• "I am an artist/teacher with an eclectic mixed media style who needs to plant her well-stocked but non-intrusive traveling studio during and possibly after a house move. I can teach anyone to incorporate creativity into their lives through art journaling and special projects. My camps are great for kids as well as grown-ups who need to free their inner artsy side. I would love to collaborate with a coffee shop or similar gathering place to offer art-making as part of the community atmosphere in addition to a little revenue for both of us. Take advantage of me now while I am in a place to negotiate. I will run an art camp at your business in exchange for small studio space."

I am a member of U-Exchange.com, which calls itself the largest free swap site on the Internet. It costs nothing to sign up and trade, and I think it is much easier to use and browse than Craigslist, although it is not yet as widely used as Craigslist. (My wife loves to shop for furniture on Craigslist and has gotten some fantastic antiques for unbelievable prices.) Here are two of my favorite real examples of trades I found offered on U-Exchange:

• "I have a private villa that sleeps 16 in Kauai. Seven-night stay valued at $3,500. You can pick your dates. I need someone to build me a deck and overhang to cover it. I will pay for the materials, I just need a contractor or builder to ensure it's done right."

• Offering a "2000 Dodge Caravan not running, or readings (intuitive, astrology, angel cards, medium, psychic, counseling, guidance) or jewelry (crystal, wrapping, hemp, repair) or holistic health counseling or nutrition" in exchange for "a running car! I have 5 children and work."

SAFE TRADING TIPS

Although I've never had any problems with any barter or trade I've ever made, I do know people who have been cheated or ripped off. Here are some tips for bartering and trading wisely:

1. Protect your address. It's probably not a good idea to offer to trade or barter gold coins or diamond jewelry and then give out your address and phone number to the world.

2. Meet strangers only in public places. If you are arranging a trade with a complete stranger, it would probably be wise to meet in a public place rather than at your home.

3. Listen to your gut. If the trade or traders seems fishy in any way, just walk away.

4. Start close to home. Launch your bartering career with people you know and trust—your family, friends, coworkers, neighbors, and Facebook friends.

5. Make sure everyone is clear on the terms. At the beginning of this chapter I mentioned that I dickered with a technician to get a lower bill. She offered to remove part of my bill in trade for attendance at

one of my Forgotten Skills classes. I had thought she meant admission for one person. But when I got around to reading the revised bill that she had sent me—and I had already verbally agreed to—the bill said she would get admission for herself and a guest. Which was fine, I had no problem with that. It just caught me by surprise for a moment because I realized I had bartered without being clear on the terms. I made a mental note to be more careful and clear in the future.

DICKERING TO SLASH THE PRICE

A couple of years ago I was in an antique store when outside sitting in the dirt and weeds was a hand-crank wheat thresher, which I have now used to thresh not only our backyard heirloom wheat but also dozens of varieties of vegetable seed (you can read more about it in the "Buying Old and Reliable" chapter of this book). This twenty-pound machine had been sitting outside so long that the price tag had been bleached blank. I took the thresher inside to the counter, having a strong suspicion that the store had no idea what it was other than some old piece of tin farm equipment. The piece turned out to be on consignment, and the clerk had to call the owner to ask the price. Even as the clerk was dialing, I had already determined two things in my mind. First, I was not going to pay more than thirty-five dollars, and second, this piece needed me like I needed it. We were going home together.

"The price is eighty-five dollars," said the clerk holding the phone.

"I'll pay thirty," I said.

The owner countered with thirty-five, and it was settled. I said I would bet the owner didn't know what it was, and I was right. I had the pleasure of telling him what he had just sold—and that I was going to put it back to work after a vacation of decades.

Dickering is more art than science. I've discovered that most people who don't dicker seem to have two reasons: first, they don't think you can do that in America or in brick-and-mortar stores, and, second, they think you have to be pushy or mean. These are both myths.

Successful dickering is about knowing when the time is right, and following some simple rules.

RIGHT PLACE, RIGHT TIME

If the person who is selling has authority to possibly negotiate a price, then the time is right. For example, you can dicker all day at the grocery store checkout, but the cashier doesn't own the items you are buying, and they have no authority to change the price. It's a pretty safe bet that no one in the store has that authority, especially if the store is a chain or a big-box store with a corporate headquarters in some faraway town. The grocery store is not going to dicker with you; neither is Walmart or Costco or any store in the mall. Wrong time, wrong place.

Here are some examples of the right time and place:

- **HIRE INDEPENDENT.** Anyone who owns their own small business is likely to at least hear you out on a proposal to negotiate a price. For our family, this has included lawn mower repairmen, plumbers, landscapers, electricians, computer repairmen, online business consultants, people who format ebooks, artists, and photographers—anyone who provides a service with their hands. The key is that they must own the business. If they are an owner, they will often dicker the price a bit, or even work with a trade. If this professional is someone that you don't know or you haven't worked with before, get the negotiated price on paper (or email) in front of them so that later the price doesn't suddenly spike. Getting the deal in writing protects both parties. Be clear—and write down—whether the set price includes parts or equipment, and any extras, and what they cost. My wife once got a friend to do a small plumbing repair job in our home in exchange for a cherry pie. (Fresh pie is a powerful negotiating tool!)

• **LOYAL CUSTOMER.** About a year ago, I needed to buy some clear plastic envelopes for my seed business. I went to the same paper goods store I always go to, and I was shocked to see the price of the envelopes had jumped 50 percent. I needed to buy several thousand envelopes. I gathered what I needed, went to the counter, and asked the cashier to get the owner. "I've bought thousands of these from you over the past several years," I said. "I could buy them online, but I'd have to wait for them to be shipped." I told him the price he had been charging me, showed him the new price, and then showed him how many I needed to buy. "This will be the largest purchase I've ever made here," I said. "But I can't afford the new price. I'm hoping you'll give me the old price." He immediately agreed.

• **NEIGHBORHOOD DEALS.** We have a neighbor who we always hire for any work with natural gas—for example, when we needed a new hot water tank installed or when we had two gas wall heaters installed or when we had to have a new stove hooked up. He knows us, we know him, and he gives us a great rate,

so we always hire him. Same with another neighbor who does small engine repair. I sell eggs, chickens, books, seeds, and vegetables to neighbors at "neighbor discount" prices, and they do the same for us. Whenever we need to buy something, we always look first to hire on our street if we can—and we always get the "neighbor discount." Be a good neighbor.

RULES FOR DICKERING

1. If you ask for a discount, be willing to pay in cash on the spot. If you need to pay with a card, you have to remember the seller has to pay a fee to the card service provider, so they are less likely to dicker on the price. Cash on the table, so to speak, can be enough by itself to sway a seller to lower their price.

2. Buy in bulk. The best price is often easier to negotiate when you can offer to buy in the largest quantity possible. If you want to can a lot of peaches, ask the farm-stand if they will take a dollar or two off the price if you buy four bushels, or ask if they will throw in a free half-bushel, which is what I usually get.

3. Bundle deals. When we decided to buy a new California king bed and mattress (I'm six feet four), we went to a locally owned furniture store and picked out the bed we wanted, and the mattress, and then asked for a discount because we were buying both at the same store. They agreed to knock several hundred dollars off the price of the mattress, especially after we mentioned the price of a similar mattress at Costco. While we were lying around on different mattresses on the sales floor, I found a pillow I really liked, but it was eighty dollars. I asked the sales guy to throw it in for free, and he didn't even hesitate.

4. Do your research. Several years ago, I needed a

new truck. I drove my old truck to the dealer who sold it to me and told them I was ready to upgrade—I wanted the same truck, just in a newer version. We negotiated a "returning customer" price and a trade-in value for my truck, which I had the salesman write down on the back of his business card. Then, to the dealer's chagrin, I said I'd need to think it over, and I left.

I left because I was serious about buying, but I had my eye on another truck from another manufacturer. I went to this competing dealer, picked the truck I wanted, and told the salesperson I was ready to buy. With a sly smile, he rushed me into a little office where he told me he could not take any discount off the price. Then I pointed out the window to the truck I had driven in, and explained that I had already been to my original dealer. I was going to buy a new truck today, I explained. I told the salesman which make and model I had chosen from their competitor, and then handed him the competing salesman's business card and showed him the price on the back of the card. I could not pay any more than what the other dealer would charge me for their truck, but I would really prefer to buy this dealer's vehicle, I explained. The salesman frowned and said he'd have to talk to his boss. He left and came back a few minutes later. No deal. His boss had said no.

"Shucks," I said. "I tried. I have to have a new truck today, so I guess I'll go to the dealer I bought my truck from."

The salesman was insistent that they had given me a great deal and that if I left now, the deal could not be guaranteed. I sadly told him I just couldn't afford anything more than what the other maker had quoted. I said good-bye politely, and I left.

But as I approached my truck in the parking lot,

the salesman came running up to me. His boss had miraculously had a change of heart. I could have the truck at the price I wanted—a five-thousand-dollar discount. I got my new truck.

It's interesting to note that I tried the same tactic when I was buying a truck years before the economy crashed, and it didn't work. But the wrecked economy had turned the car sales game into a buyer's market, and I knew it. I got the truck I really wanted at the price I really needed. And I wasn't joking—had the deal not gone through, I really was going to go back to the first dealer and buy a newer version of the truck I was driving, at the price I had already negotiated with their salesman.

5. Be assertive, not aggressive or passive. To me, the difference is based in reality and humility. The reality is that the seller has to make money to pay his or her bills, but I have bills to pay too. Another reality is that often I can't go over my budget. My reality is to negotiate the price down to my budget or find another seller who will. But reality does not give me permission to be pushy, ornery, angry, or mean. Bargains flow faster when I am pleasant. And bargains are lost when I'm passive. As long as the time and place are right, I'm not wasting anyone's time if I offer a lower but serious price. The seller won't always agree, but that's okay too. We both have our limits.

6. Be respectful. I was at a faraway farmers' market recently when I stumbled upon a guy selling landrace seeds. Most people don't even know what landrace seeds are, let alone how to use them, but I'm into that kind of thing. So I started talking to him and got details on several of his varieties, and when he saw that I knew what I was talking about, he began to ask me about my own work to save rare and pure seeds. In the end, I picked out several

Some of the author's homegrown garden seeds.

seeds to buy from him, and he said he'd just give them to me for free.

"No," I said. "I know how much work it is to grow and sell seeds. I'm going to pay full price."

And I did. He was genuinely grateful, and now I have another friend in the rare seed business—and in the work of staving off the extinction of rare seeds, you need all the expert friends, help, and sources you can get.

Being respectful means acknowledging that everyone has to make a living, that giving a discount is a sacrifice even if spending your money is a blessing to the seller. Believe me, I am grateful for each and every seed order I get at SeedRenaissance.com (subtle much?) and every book I sell. After a sale, you never know how long it will be before another customer comes along. Businesses die much more than they thrive. Being fair is something both buyer and seller have to do. When both sides are respectful, everyone benefits and goes on to enjoy their day. That's the ultimate goal anyway, isn't it?

CHAPTER 7

NO-NONSENSE HOUSEHOLD TIPS FOR SAVING MONEY

The big secret of self-reliant budgeting is this: The less you go to the grocery store, the less you spend.

Targeting the items that force you to go shopping often can mean huge savings. In my first Forgotten Skills book, I taught you all about feeding your family self-reliantly. In this chapter are my family's favorite ways to get around buying some of the other sundries you need—laundry soap, shaving razors, and toothpaste to name a few. The less you need to buy these items, the more your budget will smile—because whenever you set foot in a store, you are being targeted. Lots of science goes into tempting you to buy things you didn't have on your shopping list. I'm convinced that for every dollar we save with the following methods (which is a lot) we save two dollars on impulse purchases. Now you can too.

This is the disposable razor the author shaved with every day for 2 years using a simple sharpening technique.

SHARPENING DISPOSABLE RAZORS

Perhaps the greatest-kept secret of the modern world is that disposable razors are easy to sharpen. A single razor will last for two years of daily shaving if you sharpen it regularly, which takes about ten seconds and requires no equipment. All you have to do is run the razor backward on your dry arm. I take my razor and push it along the inside of my forearm from my elbow to my wrist, repeating about eight times. I do this once a week or so. (Make sure you are pushing backward, not pulling forward, or you will cut yourself!) This immediately and completely sharpens the razor. After about two years of sharpening, the blade is worn beyond sharpening and the razor truly becomes disposable. The Gillette razors I shave with are quite expensive, and before I learned to sharpen them, I was going through a razor every couple of months—and that was with trying to make them last painfully long. I peeked at the store the other day, and a six-pack of my replaceable razor heads costs a jaw-dropping forty-five dollars—and that doesn't even include the handle! So over two years, I saved a whopping ninety dollars by spending ten seconds every week to sharpen my razor on my arm. My current six-pack of razors will take me twelve years to use up, and I will save 540 dollars over that time! Look on my blog at CalebWarnock.blogspot.com for a video demonstration of how to sharpen your disposable razor.

NEVER BUY DISHWASHING MACHINE SOAP AGAIN

I read this tip several years ago on the fantastic *New Old School* blog of my friend Margot Hovley, and I've been using it ever since. The basic concept begins with a question: What is in dishwashing machine soap that is different from dishwashing soap? After all, dishwashing soap is super cheap, but dishwashing machine soap is super expensive. The answer? Nothing! If you never want to buy machine soap again, just put anywhere from a quarter teaspoon to a third of a teaspoon in the little soap container in your dishwasher. If your dishwasher is like mine and has two containers, just spread this tiny amount between the two. I actually don't even measure the amount, I've done it so many times. I just squirt a few drops in and start the dishwasher. If you open the dishwasher halfway through the wash cycle, you will find a foot of soap suds inside. For full disclosure, I will add that I don't put crusty dishes covered with dried food into the dishwasher at all because the dishwasher never gets them fully clean anyway, no matter what soap you are using, so I have not tested this soap method on dry, crusty dishes. (Now if I could just convince the kids that rinsing really is necessary before loading the dishwasher). This soap swap saves tons of money. A smallish bottle of dish soap costs a dollar and will do a couple hundred loads in the dishwasher. Cost per load: about a half a penny. This is one of my favorite tips of all time.

CUT YOUR CLOTHES-DRYING BILL—AND TIME—IN HALF

When I grew up, my grandmother dried all the laundry on clotheslines in the backyard. In my memory, this was true even in winter as much as was possible, and when it wasn't possible, she would bring the clothes inside to dry on racks. As she got older, my grandma started using the dryer more and the laundry lines less, but I noticed that she still air-dried her denim jeans in the house. This was because, she explained to me, denim is so thick that it takes twice as long as the rest of the clothes to dry, so if you air-dry your jeans, the rest of the laundry dries in half the time and at half the cost. Dryers are expensive to run, by the way. According to LaundryList.org, it costs up to forty cents to dry a single load in an electric tumble dryer.[1] If you run about ten loads a week, like we do, that's 192 to 240 dollars a year added to the electric bill. Air-drying your jeans can cut that in half. When you first put them on, your jeans will have that crisp, nostalgic feeling from your childhood when you used to line-dry your clothes. And if you hate that crunchy feeling, take heart—it goes away about five seconds after you put them on.

MAKE YOUR OWN TOOTHPASTE

People made their own toothpaste and tooth powder for generations before toothpaste became big business after World War II. My father has done this for years. My wife and I started out of pure frustration—the toothpaste tubes from the store kept getting smaller and smaller, and more and more expensive. We would buy toothpaste in bulk, ten packages at a time, and a month later, it would be gone. Erg! Then we started focusing on using more backyard herbs for health, and one of the first things I did was make tooth powder, which we immediately fell in love with—me because it was free (or very inexpensive), and my wife because she has always hated how overly foamy grocery store toothpaste is. Now we make our own, in bulk. A half-hour of work makes enough tooth powder or toothpaste to last a family at least a year. There are several different recipes we use, starting basic and getting more advanced. Try them all!

1. Basic Baking Soda Tooth Powder

I confess I don't prefer this recipe, but my father has used it for years. The recipe could not be more simple: wet your toothbrush, dip it in baking soda, and brush.

A jar of the author's homemade tooth powder. This jar will last 2 people a year and costs about 4 dollars to make if you have to buy the herbs.

2. Basic Peppermint Tooth Powder

This is the tooth powder we use everyday. We got this recipe from our neighbor Kirsten Skirvin, who is a certified master herbalist. Anyone should be able to get free peppermint—it grows like a weed, and lots of people have it. If you don't have it, ask for it on your local Freecycle.org group. The other two ingredients can be purchased at health food stores. A few ounces of each (total cost of about four dollars) makes enough tooth powder for two people for at least a year. I will also note that Kirsten's version of this recipe uses only a half-part of peppermint leaves, but I like mine more minty, so the recipe below is more minty. This is the basic recipe; the other recipes included here just build on this.

- 1 part ground-up dried peppermint leaves (for flavor)

- 1 part ground-up horsetail grass (contains natural silica for gentle cleaning)

- 1 part white oak bark (naturally tightens the gums)

Step 1. Using a food processor, electric grinder, or hand grinder, grind ingredients. Mix together, and you are ready to brush. If you are wondering how much each "part" of this recipe should be, they just need to be equal weights. Our local health food store sells dried herbs in two-ounce bags.

3. Slightly Foaming Tooth Powder

For this recipe, I dig the yucca root right out of our backyard, but I realize not many people have mature yucca plants in their yard. Yucca root powder is not usually carried in smaller health food stores, so if you are like me and don't have easy access to a large health food store, you'll need to order online. I only add the yucca root because I like the slight foaming action it gives. My wife prefers the basic recipe without yucca because she doesn't like foaming toothpaste.

- 1 part ground-up dried peppermint leaves (for flavor)

- 1 part ground-up horsetail grass (contains natural silica for gentle cleaning)

- 1 part white oak bark (naturally tightens the gums)

- 1 part yucca root powder (natural foaming agent) (optional—you can just use baking soda)

If you want foamier tooth powder (but still not super foamy), add:

- 1 part baking soda (be prepared, it does not taste good)

Step 1. Using a food processor, electric grinder,
or hand grinder, grind ingredients. Mix together, and you are ready to brush.

4. Whitening Toothpaste

This is my favorite—it really whitens teeth! I use this once or twice a week. Simply wet your toothbrush with hydrogen peroxide (sold in all pharmacies and most grocery stores), then dip the brush in your tooth powder. A thirty-two-ounce bottle of hydrogen peroxide—enough for years of brushing—costs one dollar at our local grocery store. A sixteen-ounce bottle costs fifty-nine cents.

If you prefer a ready-made paste, mix hydrogen peroxide to either recipe above to make a paste. If you are worried about adding this ingredient, notice that all the major toothpaste brands offer a whitening hydrogen peroxide toothpaste. In addition, our bottle of hydrogen peroxide from the grocery store says right on the label that it is used as an "oral debriding agent" which means it is swished in the mouth to clean canker sores and wounds by removing dead skin in the mouth, which can harbor bacteria (I had to look it up in a medical dictionary). So hydrogen peroxide is certainly safe for oral use. You can make the paste in amounts enough for a few weeks and keep it in a jar. As a side-note, don't be surprised if you find that little bits of dead skin on your gums have turned white after use. I can vouch that it really does "debride" the bits of what doctors and dentists call "necrotic" skin that we all have in our mouths.

LAUNDRY DETERGENT: MYSTI'S METHOD

I'm kind of miffed I didn't think of this first, especially after using dish detergent as dishwashing machine detergent for years, as mentioned earlier.

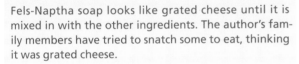

Fels-Naptha soap looks like grated cheese until it is mixed in with the other ingredients. The author's family members have tried to snatch some to eat, thinking it was grated cheese.

Grating bar soap to make laundry detergent can be done by hand or in a blender.

My stepdaughter does her laundry with dish soap instead of laundry soap because it has fewer irritants in it. She uses about a half teaspoon per regular load.

EASY HOMEMADE BULK POWDER LAUNDRY SOAP

(USE 1 TABLESPOON PER REGULAR-SIZED LAUNDRY LOAD)

This is the recipe that I prefer because it makes a huge amount, so you don't have to make it very often, and the entire recipe takes fifteen minutes to create. Walmart is the only national chain I know of that carries all of the ingredients for this recipe. They are found in the laundry aisle, usually on a bottom shelf. At this writing, Walmart's prices are $3.38 for borax, $3.24 for Super Washing Soda, and $0.97 per bar for Fels-Naptha or Zote. If I did my math right, total cost is $17.62 (if following the amount per ingredient below), and this recipes does a staggering 1,280 loads of laundry, for a cost of 1.3 cents per load. How you can beat that price, I don't know!

One tip before we get to the recipe. This is a very concentrated soap and you need to use only one level tablespoon per regular-sized laundry load (one and a half tablespoons for the biggest loads). But sometimes teens and spouses have a hard time switching to this small amount of soap. So don't give them a choice. Remove all other laundry detergents—and their scoops—from the laundry room. Put a tablespoon in with your new homemade soap, and put a sign on the bucket explaining that they need only one level tablespoon. This way, no soap is wasted by people who can't yet believe you can do laundry with so little soap!

- 1 (76-oz.) box borax
- 2 (55-oz.) boxes Arm & Hammer Super Washing Soda
- 1 bucket or pail (2 gallons or larger)
- 8 bars Fels-Naptha (or Zote)

Step 1. Pour the box of borax and the 2 boxes of

A jar of finished homemade laundry soap.

throw them in with the next 2 soap pieces. Keep going until you have shredded all 8 bars. This takes 10–12 minutes total.

NOTE: Before they are mixed into the rest of the recipe, grated Fels-Naptha looks exactly like grated yellow cheese, and grated Zote looks exactly like grated mozzarella cheese. At our house, I've had the little kids try to grab some to eat while I was making these recipes, because they think it is cheese. While you are grating, keep soap out of the reach of kids and even adults who might try to grab a bit to snack on.

Step 3. Using your hands, mix all the ingredients in the bucket. You might want to use rubber gloves for this step, but I just use my hands. The shredded soap bars need to be mixed in pretty well, so plan to spend about 2 minutes mixing with your hands. Now your laundry detergent is ready to use!

TIDE-BOOSTED BULK POWDER LAUNDRY SOAP

(USE 1 TABLESPOON PER REGULAR-SIZED LAUNDRY LOAD)

This recipe is adapted from a recipe I saw online. A lot of people swear by Tide laundry detergent. Whether that is because it is genuinely better at cleaning clothes or because of decades of savvy marketing campaigns, I'll let you decide. Either way, people like Tide, but it is pricey, and the boxes keep getting smaller. (Have you noticed? It's not just Tide. All brands seem to have shrunk their packages.) Anyway, if you want your Tide experience with homemade laundry detergent, simply add 1 small box (56 ounces) of Tide (any kind of Tide; we prefer unscented) to the bulk powder recipe above and mix it in. At this writing, the 56-ounce Tide at Walmart

washing soda into the bucket. (Pouring creates a dust, so do this outside.)

Step 2. Grate the bars of soap. There is an easy way and a hard way to do this. The hard way is to grate them on a fine-shred cheese grater by hand (or delegate to teenage boys). But trust me, grating 8 bars of soap by hand is exhausting.

HERE IS THE EASY WAY: Using a large butcher knife or chef's knife, cut each of the bars of soap into 6 or 8 pieces. (The soap is semisoft and cuts easily). Two at a time, put the pieces into your blender on the "grate" setting, pulsing a couple of times to get started. Total grating time for 2 soap pieces is about 10 seconds. Using a spatula, empty the grated soap into the bucket. You may have a couple of dime-sized chunks of soap left if your blender is cheap like ours. Simply is $7.97. This will bring your total cost per load to 1.9 cents.

POWDERED LAUNDRY DETERGENT (SMALLER BATCH)

If for whatever reason you don't want to make a big batch of the powdered detergent, you can use this recipe:

- 1½ cups borax
- 1½ cups Arm & Hammer Super Washing Soda
- 1 bar Fels-Naptha (or Zote)
- 1 large kitchen bowl

The instructions are the same as the bulk powder recipe.

BULK LIQUID LAUNDRY SOAP

(USE ½ CUP PER REGULAR-SIZED LAUNDRY LOAD)

Why make liquid laundry soap when the powdered soap is faster, easier to store, and less complex? I honestly don't know, and we don't use this recipe, but a lot of people do, including some of our extended family. I have heard some people say they don't think powdered soap dissolves correctly in the washing machine, but we've never had a problem.

Perhaps the answer is psychological. The powdered soap recipes use one tablespoon per load. In some cases—perhaps especially with children and spouses—people are really skeptical about using a single tablespoon of detergent, and they have this huge desire to use more, because they are used to using a big scoop per load. With this recipe, they get that feeling that they are using the "normal" amount of soap, and in reality, this makes them more likely to accept homemade laundry soap.

This recipe makes five gallons. If you want to make smaller batches, use one-third of the recipe amounts and water. This is a semi-gel soap and does not foam a lot. This recipe will do 160 loads, which at this writing, means it costs roughly 1.3 cents per load!

- 1 bar Fels-Naptha soap
- 1½ cups Arm & Hammer Super Washing Soda
- 1½ cups borax
- 1 (5-gallon) bucket with a lid.

Step 1. Shred the bar of soap with a cheese grater.

Step 2. Put 6 cups of water in a saucepan with soap and heat on medium until the soap melts. Add soda and borax, stirring until fully dissolved. Turn off the heat.

Step 3. Fill your bucket about a third full with hot tap water. Stir in the soap mixture from the pan. Fill the rest of the bucket with hot water and stir. Let this mix sit overnight or for a full day until it becomes a semi-gel. Cover for storage. Use ½ cup per regular-sized laundry load. (Note: if you have one of those expensive washing machines that need special soap, you probably shouldn't use this soap).

TIDE-BOOSTED BULK LIQUID LAUNDRY DETERGENT

(USE ½ CUP PER REGULAR-SIZED LAUNDRY LOAD)

The recipe is the same as the above liquid soap recipe, except you add in a 1.75–fluid ounce bottle of liquid Tide.

HOMEMADE "OXYGEN" STAIN CLEANER

Use this with your regular homemade laundry soap if your laundry is especially dirty or stained.

- ½ cup Arm & Hammer Super Washing Soda
- ½ cup hydrogen peroxide
- 1 gallon hot water

Step 1. Mix soda and peroxide with the water in a bucket.

Step 2. Let your stained clothes soak in the bucket overnight.

HOMEMADE "SPRAY & WASH" STAIN REMOVER

- 1 tsp. cream of tartar (available in the spice aisle of the grocery store)
- 1 tsp. vegetable glycerine (available at health food stores)

Step 1. Mix ingredients thoroughly.

Step 2. Rub mixture onto stain and let soak for at least 30 minutes.

CRAYON ERASER

I'm pretty sure that every home with small children ends up with crayon on the walls at some point. Here is the way to get it off: Wet a toothbrush with vinegar and scrub in gentle circles. This works because the acid in the vinegar dissolves the wax.

PORCELAIN STAIN ERASER

Sprinkle cream of tartar on your porcelain sink, tub, or toilet and scrub with a damp, non-abrasive kitchen scrubbing sponge.

MAKE YOUR OWN DRYER SHEETS

Is there anything worse than trying to fold static laundry? (Yes, I fold laundry! If your husband doesn't fold laundry, make bread, and make homemade laundry soap, I guess he's faulty. You should return him to the factory to be reset.) Or is there anything worse than going to work all day and coming home, taking off your shirt, and finding that you've been wearing a sock inside your shirt all day? (Um, of course that story is not based on personal humiliation—er, I mean, experience. Why do you ask?) The cost of dryer sheets adds up quickly, and the number of sheets in a box seems to go down every year. Making your own is super easy. There are two methods:

1. Take an old clean rag, put 3–4 drops of liquid fabric softener on it, and throw it in the dryer with your clothes. You can get a bottle of liquid fabric softener for a dollar at the dollar store, and it will last 100 or so loads using this method.

2. I invented this second method because sometimes family members would forget, when folding the laundry, that the rag was actually a dryer sheet, and the rag would not find its way back to the laundry room. So I started tying pieces of old cotton T-shirts into fist-sized knots (knotting them over and over until they were the size of a fist) and then soaking them overnight in about an eighth cup of liquid fabric softener. This was much easier because the knots could be used over and over before they

needed to be "recharged" with more fabric softener, and everyone knew that the knot was supposed to go back to the laundry room. If you don't want to soak the knots, you can put 3–4 drops on a knot each time you use the dryer.

Now for a confession. After a couple of years of use, we actually gave up this method recently at our house. It was hard to remember to keep the knots "recharged," and my wife got tired of playing static roulette—doing a load of laundry only to discover the knot had "run out" and the clothes were static-y, and she didn't like taking the time to put drops on the knot—or worse, she didn't like tracking down a knot if they had not been walked back to the laundry room. I held out for another year, using the knots whenever I did laundry, but in the meantime, my wife found a much cheaper no-name brand of fabric softener sheets, and we have switched back for now. But it still bugs me to spend money on this and to fill up the land-fill with dryer sheets. But if money gets any tighter, we might well be doing this again soon. Meanwhile,

perhaps you have a better homemade drier sheet idea. Email me at calebwarnock@yahoo.com and I might share your idea on my blog, CalebWarnock .blogspot.com.

NEVER BUY YEAST AGAIN

Use natural yeast instead of store-bought yeast for baking. Once you have a natural yeast "start," you never have to buy yeast again. We haven't purchased yeast in years, and don't ever expect to again. For a whole explanation of the health benefits of natural yeast, recipes, instructions, and how to get free natural yeast from me, see my book *The Art of Baking With Natural Yeast*, coauthored with my friend Melissa Richardson.

MINI SEED-STARTING GREENHOUSES—FOR FREE

I created these out of desperation—starting seeds indoors in winter was getting expensive. One day we bought some cookies or brownies or something at a local restaurant, and they were packed in a clear plastic container called a clamshell. I had been buying plastic seed-starting greenhouses for about ten dollars each, and it dawned on me that here was the same thing, for free. It worked perfectly. Then I got to wondering how I could stop buying those seed-starting pellets, so I started using sections of cardboard egg cartons as the pots and filling them with my own homemade compost or using a cheap bag of organic garden soil (never expensive seed-starting blends). When it is time to transplant, you just rip off the egg carton cups and plant the whole thing—the worms love the cardboard in the egg cartons, the roots grow right through the cardboard, and the whole thing composts on its own. I've also discovered that it is much easier to keep track of the varieties I've planted

These nearly free seed-starting greenhouses work better than those sold in stores.

because I can put each vegetable variety in its own greenhouse, instead of putting forty pots into one of the greenhouses from the store, and then trying to stick a marker in each pot to keep them straight.

NO MORE OYSTER SHELLS FOR BACKYARD CHICKENS

Never throw eggshells away. For years we have fed all of our eggshells back to our backyard chickens. Chickens need a lot of calcium every day to produce eggshells, and while they can get some from natural vegetation if they are free-range, most families with chickens buy oyster shell feed to keep eggshells thick. I used to do this too, until it dawned on me one day—why am I buying calcium (ground-up oyster shells) while I'm throwing calcium (egg shells) into the landfill? So I started feeding the shells to my chickens and we've done it for years now. Before you ask—no, this has not caused our chickens to start eating their own eggs, and none of them have grown a foot out of their forehead or whatever alien thing you might be afraid will happen if you add your eggshells into the kitchen vegetable and bread scraps you are already feeding them. While we are on the subject of saving time and money on chicken care, I'll just mention as I did in my first book that chickens eat snow all winter just fine—just like the birds in the sky. No electric heated waterer needed.

CLEANING SCORCHED PANS

I was teaching a class in my kitchen this spring on winter gardening and I was steaming some delicious potimarron squash to serve my students for lunch. I guess I was talking too much because the steamer ran out of water and scorched the pan, ruining the squash. When a pan is scorched, you can scrub for days and not remove the black—unless you use a paste of baking soda and warm water, or baking soda and hydrogen peroxide. I've been repeatedly amazed at how well this works. I've learned the hard way that it works best when you truly have a paste and not a wet slurry, and also when you use a nonabrasive scrubbing sponge. The scorch begins to vanish immediately, but there is usually a minute or two of scrubbing to get the whole pan clean. If the scorch mark is really stubborn, let the paste sit for a few minutes.

HAIRCUTS FOR MEN

I've been cutting my own hair for years—and no, I don't use one of those vacuum hair cutters that used to be advertised on television, and no, I don't use a buzz-cutter (two popular questions I've been asked about this). I use a pair of professional hair-cutting shears, and I don't even use a mirror anymore. The key to cutting your own hair is to start at the bottom and cut up and out—letting the hair get longer as you cut up toward the crown of your head. This allows you to trim without cutting big divots into your hair, which you can't fix. When I first started doing this years ago, there were some rough patches and my wife would have to come in and clean me up, and it would take me a half hour or forty-five minutes to cut my hair using the bathroom mirror. Today I can cut my whole head of hair in less than ten minutes without any mirror, doing it totally by feel, and I do such a good job that my wife doesn't have to clean me up. And she lets me go out in public. When I was in college, it seemed that every man I knew cut his own hair (we were all poor). My mother always cut my hair when I was growing up, and my wife cut the girls' hair when they were young. My wife cut my hair as soon as we started dating, and this went on for the first five years of our marriage, until she declared she was tired of cutting my enormously thick Scottish thatch. She told me to go to a hairdresser, but I didn't want to (I don't like strangers to touch me. Please remember this if you ever come to one of my speeches or classes). That is how I started cutting my own hair. Now I cut the grandkids' hair sometimes.

HAIRCUTS FOR WOMEN

One day my wife said she was sick of her hair and asked me to trim it. Don't fall for this, men. If I cut it, and she didn't like it, I knew the consequences would follow me to my grave! Instead, I pointed out that we do a lot of things self-sufficiently to save money, and we can afford for her to go get her hair done professionally. This will make your wife very happy. Happy wife, happy life.

DEODORANT IS FOR DUMMIES?

Perhaps I should not confess this in public, but I seem to confess everything in public, so what the heck. One day, about a year after we got married, my wife wrapped her arms around me and said, "I love you so much, and I think you are wonderful. But I don't want you to wear deodorant anymore."

Huh?

I won't lie—my first thought was "This is a trick."

Deodorant stinks like chemicals, she said. She could not stand the smell of it, and she did not want me to wear it any more. Instead, she just wanted me to take showers and smell "like a real living person."

That was a decade ago. If the public has had complaints, they've kept them to themselves. (My stepdaughters, on the other hand, have been known to say "Eww! Go take a shower!" And I obey.)

Giving up deodorant was both easy and hard. Financially it was easy. I had never liked the smell either, so that was easy. I have an allergy (like ten percent of the population) to potassium aluminium sulfate, which is the active ingredient in antiperspirant, so I had never been able to wear antiperspirant deodorant anyway. The hard part was taking the brave step of going to work that first day without it on. No one said anything if they noticed, and it was easier the second day. A week in, I had forgotten I ever wore deodorant. Soon, you're so comfortable that you start bragging about your lack of deodorant in nationally published books.

My wife, by the way, has never worn deodorant in her life. I never even knew this until she told me—and we had been married a year. She tells me that women don't smell, just men. Go figure. However, for the men reading this, you should consult your wife or girlfriend before giving up deodorant—or don't blame me for whatever may happen.

MENDING

Now that I've confessed to cutting my own hair and never wearing deodorant, I guess I can confess to anything.

I mend.

Not only that, I mend in public. I recently sewed on a shirt button in the waiting room at Jiffy Lube. Think of me as the tailor Motel Kamzoil from *Fiddler on the Roof*, only without talent.

Occasionally, I even show up in fabric stores, where I am always the only man around. Last time I was at a fabric store, it was to buy wool felt to put on the bottom of the sliders for our air hockey table. That was the mostly manly trip to the fabric store. The time before that was to buy iron-on Christmas snowflakes because my stepdaughter made my granddaughter (there is no "step" between me and my grandkids) a Christmas dress and I could not get it out of my head that the dress needed snowflakes on it. So I went and bought some, but for aesthetic reasons, my other stepdaughter drew the line at me putting them on the dress—she was afraid I'd do it ugly, so she did it herself.

I use my worn-out or ripped jeans for gardening, mostly because I'm hard on jeans anyway when I'm gardening, and it's not important that the clothes look "presentable" while I'm in the garden working off dessert. To keep ripped jeans alive one more summer, I cut up the jeans that are dead beyond hope and use the denim as patches, which I sew on with a needle and thread. As my family will tell you, my sewing is laughably bad, but again, it doesn't matter. I admit that, in the middle of a fencing project or building grow-boxes, I have worn these patchy jeans on a quick trip to the hardware store. But I'm almost always disheveled when I get to the hardware store because I'm usually in the middle of some backyard project. Everyone in the hardware store knows me, so I don't worry about it. I actually wore my patchiest pair of jeans to pick up Xander from school once, by accident. I forgot I had them on until I walked into his classroom and noticed the other parents staring at me.

What can you do?

We take baby chicks to his class every year and deliver free pumpkins to his whole class every Halloween season—and they've had field trips to my garden—so they know what I'm about. I also patch my grandsons' jeans—they go through jeans so fast because they are outside playing all summer. I had been buying them jeans, but I decided I might go broke, and if they are just using them in the backyard,

they don't have to be "presentable." So we all look "homespun" together.

I also have two stepdaughters who are fantastic seamstresses and make elaborate "real" clothes that you can wear in public. They learned to do this in high school sewing classes. Sometimes they are called upon to rescue me, as you will see next.

MAKE YOUR OWN QUILTS

I make quilts out of desperation.

When I was growing up, I never had a store-bought quilt because my grandmothers on both sides made us quilts. When I got to be an adult, they stopped making me quilts, and I had to start buying them at the store—and they were awful. My wife and I actually bought quilts once that had been sewn with what appeared to be fishing line! When the stuff started to fray and come apart, the whole quilt was scratchy and useless. Anyway, I've made quilts for twenty years. They are ugly—my wife will vouch for this. They look absolutely nothing like the quilts my grandmothers used to make—but they feel like them, and that is all that matters to me. Plus, I'm six feet four, and it's really hard to find commercial quilts that will actually keep my toes warm on a cold winter night. I make my quilts extra long. The stitching is terribly crooked, but I don't care because they are comfortable. My wife covers them with a nice quilt when she makes the bed. She calls them horribly ugly, but since she won't make me a quilt, she can't complain.

Quilting is a great project for winter, when you have to be indoors anyway. If you are a man, and you want to make a quilt—even if it's ugly—don't let the women's laughter scare you off. If you are lucky, your threat of making your own quilt will prompt someone with talent who loves you to make you a quilt (didn't work for me). If the threat doesn't work, maybe someone will take pity after they see your end result and then make you a quilt (also didn't work for me).

When my great-grandmother died, I won the family raffle to see who would get the last quilt top she had made. It was made of ugly scraps with 1960s colors, so I made a cover and used Great-Grandma's quilt as the batting. That way the family heirloom is still in use, but I don't have to look at the colors. Pretty clever, if I do say so myself. I grew up around constant sewing; my mother had a room full of sewing. If you haven't ever made a quilt, don't be intimidated—it's easy. Here are my "expert" instructions (hey, I have five or six quilts under my belt!):

Step 1. Decide what size of quilt you want, and go to the fabric store and ask for a batting (the cotton inside the quilt) in that size, and then pick cotton fabric and have them cut it a few inches larger than the batting. You'll need four lengths of fabric, because fabric comes in widths half the width of a quilt, and you need two for each side of the quilt.

Step 2. Sew two lengths together longways, and do the same with the remaining two lengths.

Step 3. Turn the fabric so it is wrong sides out and sew all the way around the square, leaving about a foot-long hole to stuff the batting into.

Step 4. Turn the quilt shell right sides out. Stuff the batting in the hole and then smooth it out inside the shell. Sew the hole shut, and then put in some stitches randomly around the quilt to hold the "sandwich" together (or stud it with yarn ties). You're done!

SILENCER FOR SQUEAKY DRAWERS

For several years, the drawers for pots and pans in our kitchen cupboards would squeak fiercely. I solved this problem by taking the drawers out and rubbing the wooden runners with beeswax. My wife was so happy! The drawers have been absolutely silent now for years.

REMOVING INK AND CRAYON FROM SUEDE OR LEATHER

My stepdaughter uses alcohol-based hand sanitizer to remove ink and crayon marks that the young kids leave on the leather seats in their new truck. She says it works remarkably well. My question is, how did the kids get to afford leather seats in their vehicles?

KITCHEN AND BATHROOM CLEANER

This is a useful general non-scratch cleaner. Mix 1 teaspoon of vinegar with 1 teaspoon of cream of tartar or baking soda and then use a rag or brush to spread this on whatever you need to clean. Let it sit for a few minutes and then wash with hot water.

CARPET-CLEANING MACHINE FLUID

My wife is adamant about this. If you rent or buy a carpet-cleaning machine, don't use any cleaner or soap in it—even the factory recommended brands. Carpet cleaning solutions leave residues on the carpet which, after the carpet is dry, will attract dirt and dust. Once you've cleaned your carpet with any kind of detergent, they seem to get dirty much faster. Instead, use only hot tap water—nothing else. If you have stubborn carpet stains, see the next suggestion.

STAIN REMOVER

I have been told that for any organic-based stain, whether on clothes or carpet, you can use hydrogen peroxide. It removes blood and dirt and most organic-based stains with ease. Simply spray hydrogen peroxide on the stain, let it sit for a few minutes, and then scrub it with a rag or brush, or in the case of carpets and rugs, go over it with a carpet cleaner.

THE RESURGENCE OF HOMEMADE DIAPERS

Diapers are expensive. I have read that the average newborn will go through nearly 2,800 diapers in their first year of life. That is six hundred dollars per year. Homemade diapers are experiencing a resurgence in popularity because of the cost and environmental issues linked to disposable diapers. My stepdaughter, Mysti Santiago, has three boys all under the age of six. She uses homemade cloth diapers exclusively. "Because they are cheaper," she said when I asked why. "That is by far the biggest reason, and because it is better for the environment. I wish I had started doing it with my first son. It makes me sick when I think about how much money I have spent on diapers that have gone into the trash."

To make the diapers, go to your local fabric store and buy a pattern, or do what my stepdaughter did and barter with a skilled friend who will make them for you. Homemade diapers work best when they are made well, she tells me. If you are not a seamstress, you can buy cloth diapers—there is a huge variety of

Zachariah, the author's year-old grandson, sporting a homemade cloth diaper.

fun patterns and colors available from craftspeople on Etsy.com, starting at about ten dollars a diaper. When your child outgrows their homemade diaper, savvy mothers join a local diaper swap, where you can either buy diapers that other people's children have outgrown (stick with me!), or you can swap or barter so that you don't have to purchase or make every diaper size as your child grows. If you do this, before using these diapers, wash them a couple of times on a hot water setting with a bit of dishwashing liquid—not laundry soap, which won't clean as well.

Here are instructions for cleaning up after your kids: For wet diapers, you wash on a warm water setting with dishwasher detergent, not laundry detergent—regular laundry detergent can cause diaper rash, my stepdaughter tells me. For a soiled diaper,

One of the happiest days in the author's life was when his grandmother, Billie Nielson, traveled to his home to see his gardens and feed his chickens. When the author was a child, he locked his grandmother in her chicken coop one day, trapping her until a neighbor heard her cries for help. His grandmother has never let him forget the story!

remove as much of the poop as possible by dunking in the toilet, and then wash the same as the wet diapers. She recommends not using bleach. Some people like to use vinegar. Air-drying in sunlight is a popular natural way to disinfect homemade diapers, she tells me.

As a side note, she also recommends using diaper-free training methods, which have dramatically reduced soiled diapers for her. With a child who is four to five months old, you set them on the toilet—using a child seat—first thing in the morning because children are likely to have a bowel movement in the morning. When these very young children get in the habit of having a bowel movement on the toilet, it reduces the amount of soiled diapers you deal with

the rest of the day, which makes cloth diapering that much easier. Diaper-free training, also called infant potty training, also makes it much easier to fully potty train your child at a much younger age. She recommends letting the young child look at books and toys while they are sitting on the toilet and you are waiting for them to go to the bathroom. There is much more information about this method online.

FINALLY, A WORD FROM MY GRANDMA

I must end this chapter by sharing the wisdom of my Grandma Nielson (pictured above). She has repeatedly and fervently shared this with all of her many grandchildren, sage wisdom for living a life free of financial worries:

"Marry rich!"

So far, not a single one of us has managed it.

Note

1. Project Laundry List, "How much energy is actually used by the clothes dryer?"

CHAPTER 8
BUYING OLD AND RELIABLE

Have you noticed that much of the brand-new "stuff" we all buy these days doesn't seem to last long?

Two decades ago, I needed a colander for draining pasta and washing vegetables. I had been to several of the usual stores to buy one, and all I could find were plastic things that were too small and too poorly made to last very long. I happened to be in a little antique store one day, and hanging up on the wall with a couple of dusty cobwebs on it was an old metal colander. It was sturdy, solid, large, and priced right. As I was paying for my find, I realized that this colander—which appeared to me to be from the 1930s—had likely given some family decades of reliable service before the next generation decided not to keep it because it was "old." So they got rid of it and went and bought—wait for it—something cheap and plastic instead.

Hmm.

After twenty years of using it, I feel confident in saying this colander and I will probably be together the rest of our lives.

Today's manufacturers have discovered that it is more profitable to sell only things that are cheap to make and don't last too long—thus luring the consumer with the cheap price and then forcing them to buy the same plastic colander over and over again. From the seller's point of view, the plastic colander is far more lucrative than a thick aluminum colander with riveted metal handles that is meant to last two or more lifetimes.

Besides, the plastic crap can be molded at high volume by impoverished Chinese workers who are paid sixty cents an hour. What's not to love?

Since the day I found my colander, I have learned that I spend a lot less when I buy old and reliable, which means used and sometimes antique. Here are some of my favorite purchases:

"PICKLES" THRESHER

In July and August, the garden harvest is in full swing, and if you can't eat out of your garden, you just aren't trying! Of course, in the self-sufficient garden, the harvest looks a little different.

Ada, the author's granddaughter, turning the antique wheat thresher that has now been put back to work after decades of neglect.

Here is a fun fact about my thresher. Scratched into the metal is this inscription: "Pickles, Sept. 24, 1954."

Hmm.

Clearly, this machine was never used to make pickles. But the word sure looks like pickles, as best as I can make out. The date is pretty clear. I've wondered if the inscription really says "picked"—which is a word used in the antiques world for "acquired." I would love to know more about this machine. I don't think it was made in the 1950s—I think it is more World War I era. At any rate, it is a gorgeous machine in my eyes, and I'm so happy to say that not only did I save it, but I've given this machine back its old job! It works flawlessly. And fast.

SOIL DRILL

Just yesterday, I was out in the garden drilling holes in the soil with a two-inch iron drill that someone had welded years ago to a six-foot iron handle, which I picked up cheap in—where else—an antique store. In my garden, I stick long, straight fruit tree branches (called water sprouts) into the ground as trellises for the pole beans. I used to have to dig a hole with the shovel to insert these deep enough to withstand the wind and kids for the whole summer season. Now I just use my soil drill. Quick and perfect. Who else but me was going to put this old tool to use? I just wish I could figure out what the farmer who originally welded it together was using it for. I'm curious as heck. Whoever they were, I like to think they would be proud that, all these years later, their handmade tool is still earning its wage.

We've been harvesting not only vegetables (which we do year-round) but also a lot of seeds. One of them is Turkey Red winter wheat. Our wheat was done (fully dry on the stalk) in the first week of July. I cut the heads off with scissors and threshed them using an antique hand-crank thresher I came across in a local antiques store (which I mentioned in an earlier chapter). The threshing went much, much faster with this great hand-crank machine, and the kids did all the cranking because they thought it was great fun. What more could I ask? The wheat is planted in autumn. It overwinters without any protection whatsoever, and our coldest nighttime temperature has been nine degrees below zero.

SHIRTS

For years, I've had to buy nice button-up shirts for work, and they were so frustrating because I would spend good money, and they would shrink, or wrinkle terribly, and they would never again look or fit as nicely as they did in the store. Out of frustration, I started buying shirts at the store for tall people so I could find a shirt that would fit right after it was washed a couple times—but then they were too big, and they cost twice as much.

Then one day I was in a thrift store buying jeans for the grandkids. They are so rough on jeans, and they grow out of them so fast, it's better to just buy them used. In the store, I walked by a shirt that I had seen brand-new not long before in a department store—the exact color and brand. Only the new shirt had been thirty-five dollars, and this one was four dollars, and it was preshrunk. I tried it on, and it fit exactly and was in perfect condition. I've washed it and washed it and it still fits perfectly. Now I buy all my work shirts at the thrift store, where I save tons of cash without any of the frustration. I've been shocked about what nice shirts I've been able to find. Now if I could just ever find any thrift store jeans in my size. . . .

Thrift store shopping spiked after the economy tanked—jumping 14.2 percent in 2009 alone and growing more than 3.5 percent between 2007 and 2012, according to IBISWorld, a company that reports on industry statistics.[1] My three-year-old granddaughter, who came out of the womb with a thing for clothes and now changes outfits about eight times a day, loves nothing more than going on a shopping spree for dresses at the thrift store. She gets ten new frilly dresses, and they only cost a couple of bucks each.

TOOTHBRUSH HOLDER

You wouldn't think this would be worth talking about, but I'm kind of proud of this one. In the years of our marriage, we've been through a few of these. Apparently toothbrush fads change, because one day I came home from the dentist (no cavities!) and the fat toothbrush wouldn't fit in the holes of this ridiculous plastic toothbrush holder that my wife bought somewhere to match the bathroom theme. (Who knew bathrooms had themes?) Anyway, I picked up the toothbrush holder out of frustration and looked in one of the holes and nearly dropped it in recoil—it was full of brown-and-black gooey mold.

Yikes.

I threw our toothbrushes away—and tried really hard not to think about what germs we'd been spreading by brushing our teeth and for how long. Yuck.

For a couple of days the toothbrushes sat on the bathroom counter. This was not sanitary either. Then I remembered that the week before I had been at an antique store and picked up a type of glass jar I had never seen before. It was squat and quite old and heavy, but it made the perfect toothbrush holder. Back when we used to buy toothpaste, my wife put the toothpaste tube in it too—which usually got left on the counter previously. Genius. We'll never have mold again in our holder. The ninety-year-old jar is easy to clean, has a wide mouth, and is made of clear glass. Best of all, we'll never, ever have to buy a toothbrush holder again. (You can read more about our homemade tooth powder and toothpaste in chapter 7.)

Here are a few of the other things in our house that we have purchased at great discounts because they were used and, often, antique (and we use all

The author's antique colander filled with early garden tomatoes.

these things every day. These are not knickknacks or display items):

- silverware
- lemon juicer
- cheese graters
- my favorite copper-bottomed spaghetti pot, which I got for one dollar at a yard sale and have used for nearly twenty years!
- carving knives, bread knives, steak knives, chef knives
- cotton, silk, and linen napkins and kitchen towels
- milk pitcher
- ceramic egg holder (in constant use!)

- a couple dozen glass vases to use as winter garden cloches

My wife and I also like to go to auctions, where the bargains could not be better. We bought the washer and dryer that we've been using for nearly a decade at auction for twelve dollars each—you read that right. With a twenty-five-dollar bid, I won my huge glass terrarium that serves as a cloche in my winter garden and is possibly the most photographed terrarium in the world. Its price if brand new: two hundred fifty dollars. I've purchased Duncan Phyfe–style tables and chairs (two complete sets, solid wood) that were so cheap I gave them away to family members in need. Here are some of the other things we have bought at auction:

- solid oak pedestal stand
- solid oak china cabinet
- nine-foot-tall antique sugar beet hoe, solid iron, bought from the Sons of the Utah Pioneers when they were holding a fundraising auction.
- oil paintings and other art
- several antique crocks
- a set of china from 1937, pieces of which have starred in numerous photo shoots for cookbooks in the publishing pipeline.

Of course, no price is better than free for a quality item. There are many things we have been gifted from family, friends, and neighbors. My favorite among these is a Harris Tweed jacket crafted from "100 percent pure Scottish wool; dyed, spun, hand-woven, and finished in the Outer Hebrides of Scotland," which is an island chain on the west Scottish coast. This jacket was given to me by my cousin-in-law and former roommate when we were both in college and he was given it and didn't want it. It fits me perfectly. Since my ancestors lived for a millennia in Scotland, I

An antique vegetable processor that can also grind dried herbs for making tooth powder.

wear this jacket with pride, never more so than when I was an adjunct professor—I looked the part. Here are some of the other things we've been gifted:

- lumber, screws, and nails
- lots of leaves for composting
- egg cartons (because we have our own chickens and we sell eggs)
- two solid wood dining buffets (both in use)
- antique player piano
- fantastic wool plaid coat from my grandfather
- pioneer chest of drawers set with mirror, painted to look like burled walnut
- side tables

CHICKEN ANTIQUES

You wouldn't think that chickens and antiques go together, but before my grandfather Phill Nielson died, I asked for one of his fifty-year-old zinc nest box sets and a zinc feeder. They were used for decades and built to last. They had been sitting in an empty coop for a decade before my wife and I dug them out. They cost us nothing, and it would have cost several hundred dollars to buy anything similar. They work perfectly. I expect they will last the rest of my life, at least. I hope they get used after my lifetime too.

Oh, there is more! Our entire barn is recycled. (I built our chicken coop into the east end of our barn.) Before I knew my wife, she had the barn dragged—literally—from a neighbor's home down the block. Voila! A free, complete barn.

Wait, there's more! (Okay, no more infomercial jokes.) We also feed our chickens old wheat, beans, and other grains from anyone who will give them to us (we get it from people who have, decades ago, put buckets of wheat and other grains in their basement out of concern for self-reliance.) We never use commercial feed.

I talked about the wonders of Freecycle.org in my first Forgotten Skills book, but I can't help but mention some of the things we have gotten for free from Freecycle since that book came out. In the past year we've gotten fifteen laying hens, three chicks, a half-dozen mature lavender plants, a casadia maker, and, best of all, more than 1,200 dollars of lumber. We gave away a waterbed that we no longer needed, along with one hundred sixty baby tomato plants from my greenhouse and other vegetable starts. Everyone benefits. If you haven't signed up for your local Freecycle group yet, what are you waiting for?

Note

1. IBISWorld, "Thrift Stores in the US: Market Research Report."

CHAPTER 9

GARDENING THEN, GARDENING NOW

THE HERITAGE DIFFERENCES

This article, by me, originally appeared in the Summer 2013 issue of Pioneer *magazine, a quarterly publication of the National Society of the Sons of Utah Pioneers.*

Our pioneer ancestors would recognize little of the techniques and methods used in today's modern backyard gardens—and they would be puzzled about why so few families garden, and why we spend so much money when we do garden.

Let's begin with the soil itself. Pioneers did not need commercial fertilizer. The soil was new, meaning it had never been mechanically disturbed. Soil health is almost entirely dependent on something called mushroom mycelium, which is a mass of thread-like branches running underground. These branches fruit by producing mushrooms. Mycelium is what allows the roots of vegetables to take up phosphorus, nitrogen, potassium, calcium, and dozens of trace nutrients necessary for healthy plants. Today's farms and gardens are deeply tilled as a method of weed control, which destroys the mycelium. Soil without mycelium is dependent on commercial fertilizers, which have been chemically designed to be taken up by plants without the aid of mycelium. When it comes to backyard gardening, I think it is safe to assume that the pioneers would marvel that we spend money to rototill our gardens, which then forces us to spend money on commercial fertilizer. The pioneers did not use chemicals of any kind.

The gardeners of pioneer times faced fewer garden pests than we do today because many of the pests we face are not native but have been accidentally imported. Their gardens were also more spread out, leaving them less vulnerable to disease and crop-specific bugs that thrive when gardens are crowded.

They did have pests—Mormon crickets are a famous example. Chickens were a primary defense, and "chicken moats" are still a mainstay concept for organic gardeners today, including me. A chicken moat simply means fencing off a garden square, and then allowing the chickens to run in a larger square around or near the garden. This way the chickens cannot get into the garden, but they can eat any bugs and pests. This method works remarkably well. It also makes it easy to feed garden trimmings to the chickens.

Free-range chickens will eat snow in winter as their water source, just like wild birds.

Pioneer families faced fewer weeds because many of the things we consider to be weeds, they considered to be wild or medicinal edibles—mallow, comfrey, lambsquarters, dandelions, purslane. Many of our modern weed plagues had not yet been accidentally let loose upon the land—they did not battle cheatgrass or bindweed, for example (imagine!). In addition, weeds are often rampant in modern gardens because of tilling. This may seem counterintuitive, but modern science has affirmed that native soils contain a natural "seed bank" in which seed stays dormant for decades. Turning the soil simply brings banked seeds to the surface, where they sprout in the warmth and light. Without tractors and tillers, the pioneers disturbed the soil much less than we do today, which itself helped keep down weed growth.

Pioneers used "leaf mold"—composted leaves—as a top dressing, as a seed-starting medium, and to create raised beds in densely clay soils, or to enrich naturally weak native soils. Animal manures were abundant. Allowing those manures to decompose turns them into a nutrient-rich soil that has been used for hundreds of years. Both leafy and animal manures heaped into piles become hot as they decompose. These hot manures were used for winter pit gardening, and heaped around cold frames and cloches to keep starving mice and voles from eating the winter harvest. Chicken manures are rich in nitrogen because chicken feathers—which naturally mix with chicken manure—are almost pure nitrogen. Backyard chickens were a symbiotic source of backyard food, providing eggs and protein along with a steady supply of soil-enriching manure. (Pioneer chickens were fed little if anything whenever the land was not covered with snow. If given access to grass and weeds, chickens will more or less feed themselves.) No part of backyard animals was wasted. Animal blood was used to enrich the soil, as were bones. "Cracked bones"—sold by the barrel—were advertised as a premier fertilizer even up to World War I in newspapers and garden magazines.

Garden seed has changed dramatically since pioneer times. The vast majority of seeds available to the public today are hybrids, which are patented and corporately owned. The twentieth century was the first time in the history of the world that seeds were legally owned by corporate entities. In pioneer times, seeds were saved from the backyard garden and actively traded, bartered, and gifted. Less often they were sold. Backyard seed-saving was widely understood and almost universally practiced. Seeds were usually purchased only when the gardener could be "sold" on the idea that the seller's seed had some strategic new benefit—and even in those cases, the pioneer gardener would have planned to purchase once, saving their own seed from that variety afterward.

Purchasing seeds each year would have been considered spendthrift. Vegetables that produce true seed at home are called open-pollinated. In pioneer times, open-pollinated seed was the only kind that existed. Today almost all seed is hybrid and/or genetically modified. Sadly, 94 percent of the varieties of garden seed that were available in catalogs in the United States in 1903 are now extinct. I work with a network of gardeners around the nation trying to save the last of the open-pollinated seed, much of which is on the verge of extinction. Open-pollinated vegetables must be isolated while flowering to be kept pure. The pioneers, who had more open space than most families today, used isolation by distance to keep their seed pure. They were also much more likely to grow single varieties of vegetables than modern backyard gardeners. Squashes, which are notoriously promiscuous, were hand-pollinated for purity in pioneer times as necessary, using muslin fabric to keep insects from reaching the squash blossoms.

A pioneer home surrounded by trees in a mountain town near the author's home.

Forcing vegetables was critical to pioneer gardeners, who did not have the luxury of modern grocery stores. I have done many book signings in Costco stores and I can always get a laugh when people ask me what my book is about if I say, "After years of intensive research, it turns out there was no Costco when the pioneers arrived—and they lived!" In truth, pioneer families forced vegetables in winter to provide themselves with fresh food. They grew "night vegetables" in their root cellars by forcing the greens of chicory, beets, and dandelions in the dark. Today, my family is the only family I know that still practices this age-old method.

The pioneers were familiar with vegetable forcing varieties that are extremely rare today, such as Amsterdam Forcing carrots, Parisienne carrots, winter lettuces, rutabaga, and perennial onions, to name a few. Glass bell jars—called cloches—and

A cold frame full of lettuce in the author's winter garden.

A bounty of fresh heirloom-variety carrots from the author's autumn garden.

glass houses were quickly common after the pioneers established themselves, just as they had been for centuries in Europe. The first documented use of a greenhouse was recorded in the first century by Emperor Tiberius of Rome, who had his servants use sheets of mineral mica to force cucumbers—the emperor's favorite—in winter. Plate-glass greenhouses were used in Rome about five hundred years after Christ and quickly spread across the civilized world. In pioneer times, millions of glass bell jars were used in the United States and Europe to force the food used to feed cities and families, along with millions of what they called "sashes"—wooden frames covered in plate glass used for winter growing. Today, forcing for true year-round eating is almost a lost art. At our house, we believe we are the last family in the United States to grow an extensive fresh winter garden, though that trend is beginning to change

because of concerns about the economy, commercial food safety, and self-sufficiency.

Root storage was the last vestige of pioneer gardening methods to be dropped in the United States. I was lucky enough to eat from the root cellars of both my grandparents and great-grandparents, who themselves grew up in a time when life without a root cellar was almost unthinkable. Row upon row of summer's bounty was preserved in glass canning jars for winter consumption, along with crocks of pickles and bins of onions, potatoes, carrots, parsnips, and more. Canning food was not a technique widely used by the pioneers, but became popular at the end of the nineteenth century. Pioneers used cellars dug well below the frost line to create a cave-like space, maintaining a constant above-freezing temperature during winter. Dirt floors allowed the heat of the earth to rise up, and the native moisture of the soil provided the humidity necessary to preserve roots. Vegetables were stored "dirt-on," which allows certain enzymes in the soil to help preserve the carrots, potatoes, and other food. The pioneers knew from experience that roots that are washed before cellaring spoil much faster.

It is also interesting to note that so-called "baking eggs" or "cooking eggs" were stored in root cellars in winter and sawdust-packed ice houses in summer. Just like roots, eggs that are not washed will keep fresh much longer in storage. This is because each egg has six thousand microscopic pores that are sealed by a natural coating when they are laid by the hen. Once an egg is washed, that coating is removed and the egg begins to spoil unless refrigerated. The pioneers stored unwashed eggs for baking, and for winter selling and trading. Eggs were sometimes preserved using the "butter" method, which meant taking them from the hen while they were still warm and coating them with butter before putting them in storage. Before modern grocery stores, so-called "baking eggs" were a precious commodity, especially in winter.

Refrigerated eggs, self-suiciding hybrid seeds, petroleum-based fertilizers, chemical pesticides and herbicides—and all the money we spend on them—would simply be unrecognizable to our ancestors. Spending hard-won cash at the grocery store while foregoing a family garden would have been unthinkable to those who were the first to make the Utah desert blossom with food and flowers.

One of the earliest-known depictions of a raised-bed garden.
This is a woodcut block print from *The Gardener's Labyrinth*,
first published in 1577.

CHAPTER 10
RAISED-BED GARDENING
CENTURIES OF FEW WEEDS AND LOTS OF FOOD

Raised beds have been used by serious gardeners for more than a thousand years. The famous French *maraichere* gardeners used compost-filled beds. Maraicheres were the "market gardeners" who fed Paris and its suburbs for centuries from their year-round gardens, called *marais*. They used intensive cultivation "to produce early crops of salads and vegetables at a season of the year when they are most likely to realise high prices in the market," wrote John Weathers in his 1909 book French Market-Gardening. "These early crops are known as 'primeurs' amongst French gardeners . . . Comparatively small areas of ground are used by growers, and it may be said that at no time during the year is the land free from crops of one kind or another. Indeed, several crops are grown on the same patch of land."[1]

According to Weathers, the maraichere method was first described in writing by a French author named La Quintinye in a book published in 1690 called *Instruction Pour les Jardins Fruitiers et Potagers*.

Some of the very earliest images (woodcut block prints) of raised-bed gardening come from *The Gardener's Labyrinth* by Thomas Hill, first published in 1577. I mention all this to show you that raised-bed gardening is not a new invention—and there is a reason why it has been used for hundreds of years.

When I'm teaching raised-bed gardening classes, I like to ask people: "What is the purpose of a raised bed?"

Most people have not thought about it. If we don't know the purpose, we don't know how to design a raised bed—and in the arid West, a raised bed designed for the wet East Coast is going to waste huge amounts of water.

There are only two purposes for raised beds. The first is to control the soil quality. The second is to control the weeds.

RAISED BEDS TO CONTROL SOIL QUALITY

The native clay soil where I live is magnificent at storing water during the scalding heat of summer—it is the ultimate water-wise soil. But it also has some significant drawbacks when it comes to gardening.

1. The soil is full of rocks, big and small. Just try to put a shovel into my backyard soil—it bites back. I am not joking when I say that I have to use a pick-axe if I want to dig a hole. This makes it impossible to grow carrots and potatoes without first dramatically improving the soil and removing lots of rocks. Any root vegetables are much more likely to be deformed as they hit rocks in their growth. The seeds of root vegetables struggle to get a good start in life because there are rocky obstacles in their way.

2. My soil is naturally alkaline, as is most soil in the western United States. This can make it difficult to sprout some vegetable seeds.

3. In the heat of summer, the topsoil is as hard as rock. In my speeches and classes, I call it "Utah's porcelain soil: better for making dinner plates than growing dinner." This can make it difficult to sprout some vegetable seeds.

4. The soil is filled with weed seeds. More on that in the next section.

Creating raised beds designed for water conservation overcomes all of these difficulties. To overcome the rock problem, you create a rock-free

Reader Question to Caleb Warnock

"I looked up your blog and really like the idea of being more self-sufficient in growing food. Our lot is 0.17 acres—is that enough space to really start making a difference growing your own food?"

ANSWER: Yes! There are many examples of people growing huge amounts of food in very small spaces. My wife and I realize we are extraordinarily lucky to have more than an acre—enough land to raise chickens, a couple cows from time to time, a big garden, and a herd of happy, healthy grandkids (our most important crop).

I have also gardened a lot of much smaller properties and even community gardens and borrowed gardens, depending on where I was living. The more you can grow, the healthier you will be, and the less money you will have to spend on food.

UrbanHomestead.org is a fascinating website about a family now famous in the homestead movement for being totally self-sufficient on a one-fifth-acre lot in urban Pasadena, California.

"We shelved our dreams of idyllic country living and 'five acres and independence' and decided to do what we could, with what we had—RIGHT NOW," they write on their website. "No one thought it was possible."[2] They produce more than seven thousand pounds of food every year, and their growing space around their home is one-tenth of an acre. Their website is inspirational and also a great resource. In their August/September 2011 issue, *Mother Earth News* magazine (one of my favorites) published a great article called "Start a 1-Acre, Self-Sufficient Homestead," which gives great information on how to be totally self-reliant on one acre. I realize this is much larger than your lot, but you can read that article to get a solid idea of what parts of that self-sufficiency plan you could fit onto your property, and what your priorities should be.

layer above the rocks. To raise the soil acidity level to something more in a happy range, you add a layer of compost. To avoid the hard soil that fights seed sprouting, you create a loamy raised layer. To let sleeping weeds lie, you create a weed-free layer. A single raised gardening bed does all of this, and this chapter will tell you how to do it at little or no cost.

RAISED BEDS TO CONTROL WEEDS

To understand how raised beds control weeds, you have to understand the basic science of Mother Nature's soil seed bank. Let's start with this sentence describing field bindweed: "Seeds may remain viable in the soil for up to 50 years."[3]

Fifty years. You can't escape morning glory. You can only awaken it.

Weeds are no fools. You can spray them, till them, solarize them, cover them, pull them, cut them—but as soon as there is water and light, new weeds will sprout. They have been designed by nature to vigorously defend themselves against the threat of eradication or extinction. A raging wildfire can literally melt sand pockets to glass because it is so hot, scorching the earth until it looks lunar, but after the first spring rain, sprouts will rise from the earth—baby trees, bushes, and weeds. This is because the topsoil is filled with a "bank" of natural seeds that will wait decades to see if they are needed. These seeds are not just in the top inch of soil, either—sometimes they are as deep as two feet. They get moved around by worms, voles, rabbits, human tilling and earth moving, and rain and frost heaving the earth. They are eternally patient, and the only way to remove them is to use a microscope to sort them out, or salt the earth. (Don't use salt in your garden. You will find my cautions on salt as a weed killer in chapter 20.)

The best way to control weeds is not to awaken the seeds—instead, let weed seeds sleep under a nice raised bed "blanket." This is what a raised bed does—it lets sleeping seeds keep sleeping. In my experience, raised beds eliminate a staggering 95 percent of weeds or more. Without raised beds, there is no way I could have a garden as large as I do. You will get a few weeds in raised beds, especially a few morning glories (bindweed), but they will be stringy and easy to pull.

BASIC "RECIPE" FOR BUILDING RAISED BEDS

Here is the basic recipe, explained in detail:

1. Build a frame.

2. Line the ground inside the frame.

3. Fill the frame with filler.

4. Put a "topping" on the filler

5. Plant your seeds and garden!

This photo shows the layers of a raised bed under construction. Note the paper used as liner to block weeds in the native soil, covered with a layer of leaves.

The same raised bed finished with a thin layer of compost on top, which is used to start seeds.

WHEN TO BUILD RAISED BED BOXES

I almost hesitate to answer the question of when to build your raised beds. Ideally you build them in the fall, so they have time to begin decomposing over winter. Plus, autumn provides great weather for working outdoors, and there seems to be more time because other garden tasks are winding down. But I know from everyone who has been to my classes that most gardeners are not thinking of building boxes until spring rolls around. Spring and late winter work great too.

HOW LONG, HOW WIDE?

I strongly suggest you don't build raised boxes wider than the reach of your arm. The wider they are, the harder they are to plant, harvest, and weed (even if weeding is drastically reduced). My beds are long—up to fifty feet long without crosspieces of wood. I have found that these long boxes begin to bow out in the middle under the weight of wet soil, and they are slowly expanding out into my pathway. For all my new boxes, I build rectangles that are no bigger than eight feet long and three feet wide. The height of your boxes is a bigger subject and will be covered below.

THE GROUND: DECIDING WHERE TO PUT RAISED BEDS

You can put your beds in any blank, sunny space. But the question I get asked most often about building a raised bed is, can I build it on top of grass, or do I need to till up the grass? No need to kill the grass—the raised bed will do it for you, as I will explain in "The Filler" section of this chapter.

A bigger question, which I also get asked a lot, is what if you have used weed-and-feed or other chemicals or nonorganic fertilizers on your grass, and you would now like to convert that land to an organic vegetable garden? The answer is based on the concept of good, better, and best. If you have used a chemical, but now you want to convert that space to an organic garden, I would rather see you gardening than waiting. The common consensus in the gardening world seems to be that you could consider the garden space "organic" after three years of no chemical use—but do you want to wait three years? You could dig the soil out and replace it with organic soil, but that is backbreaking, time consuming, and expensive. Most of all, I have found it to be prohibitive to most people, meaning they think of all that work and decide to forget the whole project.

My answer is that it is better to get started with your new garden now, even if you have previously sprayed glyphosate (Roundup chemical weed killer), even if you have used petrochemical fertilizers on that spot. Now you want to go in a new, healthier direction, and I think you should start in the way you want to continue. Years ago, based on recommendations from our local garden experts at the university extension service, I too sprayed Roundup for a year or two. But using a chemical bothered me, the expense bothered me, and, most of all, the notion that it "had to be done this way" bothered me. I felt sure that the push to spray was motivated by money and pushed heavily by the companies making huge profits—and I was right. I decided to get educated, and when I knew the truth, I said good-bye to anyone who insisted that gardens only work when you spend cash on chemicals. Good riddance! So if you are now at a place in your life where you want to start on a

healthier, more sustainable path, just start. Don't wait. Opportunity is not a lengthy visitor.

THE FRAME

Your raised bed frame should be made of untreated wood and should be free. In my garden I use regular two-by-four pine lumber for everything except the beds for potatoes and carrots, which must be deeper. (I grow my potatoes in straw. You can read about that in my first Forgotten Skills book).

No matter where you live, every day thousands of dollars of used but still useful lumber is thrown away. To get free wood to build your frames, ask friends and neighbors. Ask at church, at school. Or

use Freecycle.org or the free section of Craig's List to ask for clean used lumber. I have not paid for a single stick of the lumber I have used to build my extensive raised bed garden. You shouldn't either.

RAISED-BED GARDENING QUESTIONS AND ANSWERS

I've taught raised-bed gardening classes enough to know you are likely brimming with questions. Here are common questions and their answers:

QUESTION: Won't untreated lumber rot and fall apart?

ANSWER: Probably eventually. None of mine has yet, and it's been in the garden for years. If it does, frames are quick and easy to make, as I will explain.

QUESTION: Can we use anything else beyond free lumber?

ANSWER: Some people, including my stepdaughter, insist on buying the pretty white vinyl raised bed boxes from the hardware store. (Beware, however—the vinyl is prone to cracking and has a short life span in my observation). My raised bed boxes are beautiful to me, but a certain blogger made it clear that my boxes are not beautiful to everyone. I think they are even more beautiful for the fact that they are free, but I don't live in an urban suburb with lots of judgmental neighbors or pressure to make my garden look like Martha Stewart visited with a fairy godmother wand. If aesthetics are more important to you than doing it for free, then buy the fancy boxes, or buy redwood lumber to make your boxes. As long as you get gardening, and you are happy with your boxes, what material you use is, well, immaterial to me. You can use stone to make your frames. You can use bricks. Don't use concrete, which is a natural desiccant, meaning it draws water from living tissue and can kill plants and vegetables.

QUESTION: Can I use railroad ties?

ANSWER: I am whole-heartedly against using creosote-preserved railroad ties, but lots of people are not as concerned about the potential of creosote to cause cancer—I've been pounded down on Facebook about this one. A lot of people have had railroad ties in their yards for decades—including us (they were there before I moved here)—and have seen no ill effects, and they think my concerns are silly. But the concern is real. The US Environmental Protection Agency's "Preliminary Risk Assessment for Creosote" says this: "Creosote is a possible human carcinogen and has no registered residential uses."[4]

Again I return to this—be educated, use what makes you excited to garden, and spend what makes you happy. In the end, the most important thing is that you get started.

QUESTION: Your raised beds are hardly raised at all. Why are they so short?

ANSWER: A great question, and the answer is important. If your climate is arid, your raised beds should be as low as possible. This will allow the roots of your plants to access the native soil, which naturally conserves water in summer heat. Native soil "banks" water. You can demonstrate this with an easy experiment. Take two identical plants and plant one in the ground, and another in a pot. Pour a cup of water on both and don't water again. Instead, count the days until the plants begin to wilt. The plant in the pot will get dry much faster than the plant in the ground. This is because the soil in the pot has more surface area exposed to the air, which sucks moisture from the soil in dry climates like the arid West. Plants with roots in native soil have access to the water "bank" and will last much longer in heat and drought.

If your climate is wet, raised beds will help prevent root rot and diseases associated with undrained soil.

The height of your raised beds should depend entirely on the climate where you live. If you live in the East or on the West Coast of the United States—or some place where it rains a lot in Canada (hello to all the Canadian fans of my books)—then taller raised beds will work best for you because drainage to prevent root rot will be one of your primary concerns. But where I live at five thousand feet in the Rocky Mountain deserts of the West, drainage is something we must try to prevent. Every drop of water is precious and increasingly expensive.

As I write this, we are in a drought and water supplies all over my county are low. Our city, along with all the neighboring cities, has ordered outdoor watering restrictions, and the temperature has just soared into the triple digits for the first time this summer (it's late June). I water my mature garden once every eight to ten days, which is the correct watering schedule for vegetable gardens.

Our native soil is clay for a reason. Clay holds water in heat. If our native soil were not clay, the area where I live could only be a windswept sand dune (and we have those nearby too). Luckily, over thousands of years, the sand has been swept into dunes by the wind, leaving the water-grabbing clay behind. Loamy raised bed garden soil drains rapidly, and every inch of loam I put into a raised bed box is going to require exponentially more water to keep it wet—for two reasons. First, water follows gravity, and loam drains quickly. Second, there is no humidity to speak of where I live, so the very air sucks moisture from the soil. Raised bed boxes have more surface area exposed to the brutal air because they have sides, so they get sucked dry even faster than the ground. So for dry climates, raised beds work best when they are as short as possible.

As a side note, a lot of people get frustrated where I live about hanging flower pots. Every nursery and hardware center sells them, and they are not cheap, but they don't work where I live unless you faithfully soak them in water twice a day in July and August. Hanging baskets in a desert are ridiculous—per square inch, they demand far more water than any other type of gardening. The dry air greedily sucks the moisture out of them, and if you are not vigilant, your thirty-dollar basket of color is dead, almost within hours.

The solution to all this, of course, is to work with Mother Nature, not against her.

THE LINING

Lining the bottom of your frame is essential for keeping out weeds. You can use organic weed fabric, which is made out of paper and meant to dissolve within a year. But that costs money. Here are some free or nearly free solutions:

- Paper bags from the grocery store. Hopefully your local grocery store offers you a choice of paper or plastic, like mine does. I always choose paper because these paper bags are compostable—most of them are labeled as such right on the bottom. They make great lining material for new raised garden beds.

- Newspaper. Ink by law is nontoxic and vegetable based, so you don't have to worry about the ink. However, glossy newspaper has been treated with a chemical that you don't want in your garden, so be sure to use only newspaper that does not have a gloss. You can get newspapers from your local Freecycle.org group, ask your friends and neighbors, or ask on Facebook.

- Newspaper rolls. Newsprint comes in huge rolls, and when the rolls get to the end, they are replaced. Most newspaper offices will either give these end-rolls away or sell them quite cheap.

- Craft paper. Brown craft paper makes a great liner and can be purchased in rolls fairly cheaply or even at dollar stores.

Don't use any liner that contains glue or chemicals. Cardboard, for example, is glued together, so you don't want to use any cardboard unless you know the glue is organic (I haven't found any yet). Cereal boxes and shoe boxes have a shine on them, which is a chemical, so you don't want to use them.

One more benefit of using paper to line the bottom of your garden boxes—worms love wet paper, and they will flock to it.

QUESTION: How much liner should I use?

ANSWER: A lot. I suggest at least a quarter inch of liner, which is a lot. However, I have recently tested store-bought organic weed barrier. I put a single thin layer under some raised bed boxes I built in my pasture. Amazingly, this thin layer kept out all the weeds—and the weeds were thick and deep. This suggests to me that we could use an even thinner layer of newspaper or craft paper and be okay. But I usually use a thicker layer, to be safe.

To avoid weeds creeping in from the edges, make sure your liner extends out farther than your garden box.

QUESTION: Can I just build my boxes on cement? Or can I line my boxes with landscape pavers to prevent weeds?

ANSWER: No and no. Cement is a natural desiccant, meaning it pulls moisture out of plants, which can damage or kill them. This would also block the roots from reaching the native soil, which is what you want them to do if you live in an arid area so you don't have to water so much.

QUESTION: Can I line my box with gravel for drainage?

ANSWER: I wouldn't. To grow root vegetables in a box lined with gravel, your box would have to be filled with enough soil to make sure that your roots don't reach the gravel. As discussed earlier, the higher your box is, the more water it is going to use.

THE FILLER

Filling your raised box should not cost you a dime. The best fillers are pine needles, tree leaves, clean grass clippings, straw, and hay. My wife and I ask our neighbors to drop their bagged leaves on our front lawn every fall—what we don't use for filling new raised beds goes into the compost pile. I also ask for leaves on my local Freecycle.org group and at church. And when I'm driving around locally in autumn, if I see someone with a bunch of bags filled with leaves on their front lawn, I always stop and ask if I can load them up, and they always say yes. We get pine needles the same way, as well as getting them from our own pine trees. I accept grass clipping from friends and neighbors as long as they have not used chemicals on their lawns. You can get old straw and hay from local farmers, and there is always a lot of it around after Halloween that people have been using for porch decorations. Just stop and ask for it. I even get it from stores that use it in displays in the fall and then don't want it anymore. Where I live, most hay is not sprayed with chemicals. However, certified weed-free hay has been sprayed with pesticide.

QUESTION: How deep do I layer in the filler?

ANSWER: I recommend that you fill the box to the top, and then some. At least four inches above the top. You'll want to walk or jump on your box after you've added the filler to tamp it down as much as possible, but all this organic material is still going to begin to "melt" over the next few months, so if you fill your box at least four inches above the top, it will be about right by the time the filler has decomposed into compost.

QUESTION: How on earth am I going to be able to grow anything in a box made of two-by-fours and filled with pine needles (and so on)?

ANSWER: Have faith. I know it seems like failure waiting to happen, but it is not. I've done this many times. Once you begin to water your boxes, the filler will immediately begin to decompose and slowly compact. The pine needles, leaves, grass clippings, hay, or straw will absorb and hold water, and the roots of the baby plants will happily grow down into it. As you watch all this happen—and as your plants thrive growing in a bed of pine needles—you will think to yourself, "That Caleb Warnock—humble, wise, and charming—sure knows his stuff!" And you will be right, natch.

QUESTION: If the filler has to decompose, isn't spring too late? Does my new box have to sit for a year before I can use it?

ANSWER: This is my favorite question because the answer astonishes people. No! I have expanded my garden every year for years now, and at this very moment in late June, I have a dozen brand-new raised beds that are filled with nothing but pine needles, and the squash in them are growing great. I do this every year because time seems to escape me too. I usually try to get my beds built and filled in the fall, yet last fall I got the beds built but not filled. In fact, the beds did not get filled until it was time to plant. Despite being just filled with pine needles instead of soil, everything grows fine. I've used just-filled beds for many years, and I've never had a problem.

QUESTION: What if I can't find any free filler or I just want to buy soil to fill my boxes?

ANSWER: Your money, your life. If you can't find any free filler, where do you live? I can't imagine not being able to find people who want to get rid of leaves and grass clippings. If you really want to fill your boxes with soil for some reason, make sure you get soil or compost that is certified weed-free—otherwise you are just wasting your time. (Certified weed-free means it says on the package that the soil or compost has been heated to kill weed seeds.)

QUESTION: I have already built my boxes and filled them with soil or compost I purchased. What do I do?

ANSWER: Depends. Perhaps nothing—if the boxes work, run with them. If you built deep boxes (and you probably did), the next question is how many do you need? If you are going to expand next year, save the deep boxes for growing potatoes and carrots, and build new shallow boxes when you expand. Then, to fill your new shallow boxes, use the soil or compost from your deep boxes, and then grow potatoes in straw in your empty deep boxes. (For instructions on growing potatoes in straw instead of soil, see my first Forgotten Skills book.)

QUESTION: What if I already filled my boxes with topsoil I bought in bulk, and it was not weed-free and now my box is filled with weeds.

ANSWER: The best answer is to get my recipe for Caleb Warnock's Guaranteed Edible Weed Killer (see the weed killer section of this chapter for

The author's grandson, Xander, helps fill a deep box with shredded paper and straw, which will decompose to become compost. The finished compost will then be used to grow carrots.

information). You could also try this: Soak the soil in the box with vinegar—and I mean soak—and then cover the whole box with plastic to "solarize" it for a couple of weeks by heating it as hot as you can get it with the sun. Between the heat of the sun trapped by the plastic and the acid from the vinegar, you should kill not only all the weeds but also most of the seeds too. If you have naturally alkaline soil (like the western United States), then vinegar is great for your soil, so you don't have to worry about that. If your soil is already acidic, vinegar won't hurt it.

QUESTION: I can get cheap compost from my county green waste program or sewer district. It's made out of shredded branches and green waste. Can't I just use that as filler?

ANSWER: Depends. At my sewer district, the compost includes the human waste too, and therefore it has every medicine in it that everyone is taking, plus who knows what else. They will tell you, if you ask, that their compost is not recommended for vegetable gardening for this reason. The county just north of mine, however, has chosen to send their human sludge to the landfill and their compost is made only of green waste. This could work, but green waste is made up of a lot of things—tree branches, grass clippings, leaves, and weeds. If heated to the correct temperature, the composting process should kill the weed seeds, but just to be safe, you might want to buy some and put it in a pile in your garden for a couple of weeks, water it well, and see whether or not it sprouts lots of weeds. If it doesn't—and if you have confirmed that it does not have human waste sludge in it—then you could use it as filler. And it is cheap: about twenty dollars for a cubic yard.

THE TOPPING

After you have heaped your raised bed so that it is more than full with filler, you will need to put a half-inch layer of compost on top. Or a large handful of compost in every spot you intend to plant seeds. (You can use your own homemade compost, or you can get a bag of organic compost from your hardware store, which costs about three dollars where I live.) This layer is just for starting your vegetable seeds in. I know it doesn't seem like enough, and you will be tempted to put a lot more compost on, but I have done this many times—all you need is just enough to bury your seeds and hold enough water to get them started. It works. I promise.

PLANTING YOUR NEW BOX

Plant and water as you would any garden.

QUESTION: What about corn? It seems like corn would blow over in the wind if it were in a loamy raised bed filled with needles or leaves.

ANSWER: If your box is shallow per my recommendation, the roots of corn can reach the native soil and should be fine. To be extra sure, divot a hole into your filler, fill the hole with a handful of compost, and plant a couple of corn seeds in each hole. The hole should be half as deep as your shallow box. Or just fill your box halfway with filler, spread a half inch of compost, spread your seed, and then fill the box with the other half of your filler. Either way, your corn will be close enough to the native soil to establish a good root hold to withstand the wind—if you don't overwater. Once it is established, corn only needs to be watered every eight to ten days, just like the rest of the garden. If you have problems with the wind blowing over your corn, that is a sure sign that you are overwatering your garden.

QUESTION: Can I plant beets, onions, and root vegetables in my new box?

ANSWER: Yes. They will do fine.

QUESTION: You said carrots and potatoes should be in a deep box. How deep? Do I fill it differently?

ANSWER: For carrots and potatoes, your box will need to be ten to twelve inches deep.

For carrots:

The entire box will need to be filled with rock-free compost if you want straight, thick carrots. Better yet, use a mix of half compost and half sand. Make sure the sand and compost are well mixed.

For potatoes:

I strongly recommend growing potatoes in either straw or a layer of compost with straw on top. My recent garden tests have proven that you will get double the yield of potatoes if you put the seed potatoes (or peels with eyes) in the bottom of the box and cover them with a mix of half sand and half compost, enough to fill the bottom third of the box. Fill the rest with straw.

QUESTION: How do I rotate my carrots and potatoes if they have to stay in my tall raised beds?

ANSWER: Rotating where you plant your vegetables each year helps reduce disease in the garden. Gardens should be rotated on a four-year schedule or longer, meaning you don't plant the same type of vegetable in the same spot for at least four years. When my straw potatoes are done, I move the straw to the compost pit. Then I fill the potato bed up so I can use it to grow carrots, filling the bed with a new mix of half compost and half sand, using compost I make on my own property. To rotate my potatoes into my former carrot bed, I remove the top two-thirds of the compost and use it to top off other beds or to top off new beds. I plant my potatoes in the bottom third of the compost that is left and then fill the rest with straw. Especially with potatoes, it is essential to rotate them every year so you don't encourage disease to build up in the soil—and it will, if you don't rotate.

WATERING YOUR RAISED BOX

After filling your box, water it once or twice to get the decomposition process started before you plant your seeds.

I use two methods for watering my boxes. The first is to water them by hand with the hose. This is my favorite method because it is a relaxing way to spend a summer evening and also because it allows me to keep water off my pathways, which goes a long way toward keeping weeds off my pathways.

The second method for watering my boxes is using a single overhead oscillating sprinkler. Mine cost ten dollars at the local hardware store, and it waters the entire garden space. I screwed the sprinkler onto the top of a four-by-four piece of lumber that I stuck in the ground so it was about four feet high. This allows the water to get over the corn and every other tall vegetable as the summer goes on. Then I water about once every eight to ten days overnight—a good deep watering. Squash plants and others should generally not be overhead-watered, but I have found that as long as I water overnight, the sun dries the leaves in the morning, and I've had no problems. I do eventually get powdery mildew, but I ultimately get it even when I water at ground level, and overhead watering once every ten days does not make the powdery mildew come earlier, in my experience.

Of course, you water seeds differently than you water a mature garden. Seeds should be watered every day until they sprout and each day for the first two days after sprouting. Then begin to skip a day in succession. For example, on the third day after your seeds have sprouted, don't water. Water on the fourth day but not the fifth or sixth day. Water on the

seventh day, then don't water for three days. Water, then don't water for four days. Water, then don't water for five days. Follow this pattern until you are at eight to ten days between waterings. Of course, this pattern assumes you are getting no rain. If you get a good rain, you can start your day count over again. As I write this, we've had some rare heavy summer rainstorms, and I haven't had to water my garden in nearly a month—which is the first time I've not had to water in July in my whole life!

QUESTION: What about using drip lines? Everyone uses drip lines. They are so water wise, surely you use them. (Followed by more inane gushing about the wonders of drip lines. Can you see where this is going?)

ANSWER: Never. I hate drip lines, and I can't believe people are still using them, although their popularity has begun to fall off dramatically. This is because drip lines clog so easily—even the new supposedly less cloggy kind—and they cost

hundreds of dollars to install. You often don't know you have a clog until your plants begin to die. Clogs are time-consuming to clean out, so most people simply go buy a new drip-head, costing them even more money. I don't understand why people use drip lines. An oscillating sprinkler costs ten dollars and waters the entire garden!

QUESTION: Will my garden make it ten days without water? Won't it die?

ANSWER: Your garden will survive ten days without water, with two exceptions. First, if your raised beds are tall, you are going to have to water more often. (Even my carrots and potatoes in twelve-inch-tall beds get watered only every eight to ten days, however, and I've had no problems with them.) Second, if your temperature goes above 110-ish degrees, you are going to need to water about every five days.

There is one single reason that most people overwater their garden, and that is the pepo species of squash. About half of the pepo varieties—including summer squashes and zucchinis and many orange pumpkins—use a unique cooling system when the temperature gets over 90 degrees or so. Even a few non-pepos exhibit this trait. They pant. Kind of like a dog pants its tongue in the heat. Except a panting squash looks wilted. People see these wilted squash, and they are sure their garden is dying, so they turn on the water. The problem is, no matter how much you water, they will keep panting in the heat and you will keep thinking they are dying.

Luckily, I have noticed that there is an easy way to discern between a happily panting pepo and a squash that is truly dying of thirst. Simply go out to your garden in the afternoon and observe which squash are wilted. Then, return at dusk, just before the sun sets. Panting pepos will have begun to visibly unwilt themselves in the last half hour of daylight as the temperature cools, even though they might not be totally unwilted by dark. (They will be completely unwilted when morning arrives.) Truly thirsty squash will still be wilted at sunset. If they are wilted, then you know you need to water—and I recommend a heavy overnight watering, and then leave them alone for eight to ten days, as I said.

EDIBLE (CHEMICAL-FREE) WEED KILLER FOR GARDEN PATHWAYS

Unfortunately, weeds still grow in the pathways around raised beds, which has been a source of frustration for me for years. So I decided to do something about it. Something I believe is truly revolutionary. After years of work, I am pleased to say that I have formulated an entirely edible weed killer that is guaranteed to kill all backyard weeds—including the roots—in one application when applied as directed.

My belief is that this recipe has the potential to change the world. With this recipe, I cannot see any reason to use any chemical weed killer.

I had been very close to creating a recipe for edible weed killer for a couple of years, and I had been working feverishly since early spring in 2013 to perfect this recipe. After giving speeches to thousands of people because of my books, the biggest request from audiences has been a safe and chemical-free recipe for killing weeds. People have told me they want to give up using Monsanto's Roundup and its generic versions because of concerns about expense and long-term effects.

I had been certain for years that it was possible to create an all-natural weed killer that could be guaranteed to work as well as all commercial weed killers, at a much lower price, with no environmental or chemical risks. My only requirement was that the recipe be entirely edible because I'm not going to use anything in my garden that isn't safe to put in my mouth. My years of work had come tantalizingly close. In early 2013, the final two puzzle pieces clicked together.

First, master herbalist Kirsten Skirvin was teaching a class at my home when she said this: "Whenever there is a problem caused by nature, the natural solution is always only a few feet away." I admit it sounded like hocus-pocus to me. My first inclination was to apologize to those who had paid to be in the class. But Kirsten is not a fly-by-night herbalist. She has more than two decades of experience. I decided to be quiet and put her words to the test. She was talking about cuts, burns, and stings—not killing weeds. Nevertheless, as I began to test her theory, I began to see that it was true. And I started to wonder how it could be applied to weeds.

The second puzzle piece clicked for me while I was teaching a class earlier this year. Someone asked me a question about something completely unrelated to killing weeds, and I answered the question—and realized in that instant that the answer to my weed killer had been staring me in the face for three years. I knew immediately that I had found a recipe I could guarantee, at last. After that breakthrough, I tested and tested. I figured out the exact vegetable-based formula. The most difficult and frustrating part was figuring out how to apply it correctly. As it turns out, the way the weed killer is applied makes all the difference in the world.

My weed killer

- Is entirely edible. The recipe doubles as a super-healthy salad dressing, which is how I would suggest you eat it.

- Kills all common backyard weeds in one application when applied as directed.

- Is guaranteed safe for pets, bees, and insects as long as you don't apply it directly on them.

- Is safe and even beneficial for garden soil.

- Is safe for use around children and is safe for the person applying the weed killer. (Except that you could hurt your eyes if you got it directly in your eyes. Do not get the formula in your eyes.)

- Where I live, the ingredients, when purchased at a grocery store, cost just less than $3.50 per gallon to make at home. One gallon will kill one hundred to four hundred square feet of weeds, depending on their height and density.

- Can be all-natural and 100 percent organic, depending on the quality of vegetables you purchase to make it.

- Will kill living weeds of all ages and is

The author worked for 5 years to perfect an all-natural, edible recipe for weed killer.

guaranteed to kill field bindweed, mallow, cheatgrass, dandelions, dock, lawn grass, clover, broadleaf grass, perennial weeds, and all common backyard weeds in a single application when used as directed.

- Does not use salt and will not affect future plantings or have any negative or long-term affect on your soil or garden.

- Takes less than five minutes to make. You will need a blender.

- Will also kill vegetables, berry bushes, flowers, and shrubs if applied directly on them. Apply only to plants you wish to kill. This weed killer may also kill insects if applied directly on them.

It is no exaggeration when I say that creating this formula has required five years of work, thousands of dollars, hundreds of experiments, and hundreds of hours of testing. Because of all this expense and effort, I cannot give this recipe away. The recipe is available for purchase at SeedRenaissance.com. You need only to purchase the recipe once to use it for your lifetime. My recipe is guaranteed to work, with a thirty-day money-back guarantee.

OVERWINTERING YOUR RAISED BEDS

Because I have written a popular book about how to garden in winter without artificial heat or electricity in any climate, *Backyard Winter Gardening*, I get asked a lot whether you can use the raised beds you used in summer for winter gardening too. The answer is yes. I put cold frames and cloches on my shallow raised beds for lots of happy, fresh winter eating.

If you don't want to winter garden (What's wrong with you? It's so easy—no bugs, no heat, no work, almost no watering—just picking fresh food!) then I recommend, if you live in the western United States, that you plant peas in every available garden space in the fall. Peas fix nitrogen in the soil, and most soil in the West is always nitrogen deficient. Soils in the East are nitrogen deficient in certain circumstances based on rainfall and other factors. (Sorry, Canadian friends. I have no idea what goes on up there in your soil. Email me and educate me at calebwarnock @yahoo.com.) Even if your pea plants never produce peas, they will still fix nitrogen in your soil. And if you use the early-variety peas available at my site, SeedRenaissance.com, you will get to harvest peas in the fall too.

THE SECOND YEAR AND ONWARD

The soil level in your raised beds will have sunk fairly dramatically after the first year of use, as all the air in your filler has left and the organic matter composts and decomposes. This is why I recommend you mound up your filler at least four inches higher than your frame when you first fill your bed. If your soil level is low in future years, add a layer of compost to the top of the bed. People ask me if they need to refill or rebuild their beds each year. No. Raised beds are permanent. Just top them off with fresh compost if needed. Otherwise, just use them over and over again.

BONUS QUESTIONS

When I was nearly done writing this chapter, I remembered one more common question that I needed to go back and answer. And then it dawned on me that I should post a message on my Caleb Warnock author Facebook page—hint, if you are on Facebook, you should join me—and ask what questions people might have, to see if there were any I hadn't thought of. Good thing I did because I got a bunch. Here they are, with answers:

QUESTION: Can either perlite or vermiculite be used on the top?

ANSWER: Yes. Perlite is not a chemical. It is actually a form of volcanic glass that becomes permanently light and fluffy and stores water nicely after being heated. It is organic, and you can use it in raised beds if you want to buy it. It's actually pretty cheap, and a small bag will lighten the soil in a raised bed. I use it occasionally. Vermiculite is a water-friendly (hydrous) mineral in the silica (glass) family that is flaky and light and helps lighten soil and hold water. It usually comes from a mine. It is organic and I use it in small amounts. It is not expensive.

Potato plants emerging from the deep raised boxes filled with straw in the author's garden.

QUESTION: Are there good fillers for taller raised bed gardens?

ANSWER: Great question. I had an elderly neighbor who had a raised bed built for her that was quite tall because it was no longer feasible for her to kneel down and garden. She filled hers totally with purchased soil. In my geothermal greenhouse, my raised beds are five feet tall, but they are built into the walls underground and connected directly to the native soil outside the greenhouse. The bottom half of them is filled with rock, and the top half is filled with my own compost. I also use shredded paper and paper egg cartons as free filler in both the beds and pots in my greenhouse. Of course you could just fill a tall box full with any of the free fillers listed in the fillers section of this chapter.

QUESTION: How do I protect raised beds from kids?

ANSWER: Put a fence around your garden with a locking gate. That's what I did. The little kids are allowed to be in the garden freely as long as I am in the garden, but when I'm not there, no one is allowed inside. Same answer for dogs.

QUESTION: Are there any garden vegetables that won't do well in a raised bed?

ANSWER: I have grown everything in raised beds. I do use some regular garden ground too, but man, that is a lot of weeding. Wheat does best in clay soil, and I grow my winter wheat in my pathways and my summer wheat in raised boxes filled with native clay soil, which I dug up from more than two feet below ground so I could get it as free of weed seed as possible.

QUESTION: How do I keep my tomato cages from tipping over in the wind and breaking my precious plants off at the base of the stem? *Snap.*

ANSWER: What an interesting question! We have ferocious winds here (up to ninety miles per hour on occasion), and this has never happened to me. To be honest, I strongly suspect your problem was more likely to have been caused by a startled deer that bolted when it heard a dog or something. When we first put up our new fence, the deer crashed into it three times in the night, doing real damage to the fence—and surely the deer—before word got around in the deer community. (I guess. At any rate, it stopped happening.) If it really was wind, I would suggest getting one of those tomato cages made out of concrete-reinforcing wire mesh, which is heavy-gauge wire netting.

QUESTION: Can I just use regular soil?

ANSWER: Nope. The regular soil is full of weed seeds, which defeats the purpose of a raised bed. If you use regular soil, your raised bed will have just as many weeds as your ground does.

QUESTION: How sturdy do I have to make the raised boxes?

ANSWER: Use regular two-by-fours. I wouldn't use one-inch-thick pine boards because they will warp pretty quickly.

QUESTION: Do I really need to make sturdy boxes with corner posts and all that?

ANSWER: My twelve-inch-deep boxes have corner posts because they are made of stacked two-by-fours, which were free. I could have used twelve-inch boards, but I didn't have any for free at the time, and they warp easily. Regular shallow beds don't need corner posts for support. Only beds about six inches or higher need corner supports. Good question.

QUESTION: Can I just heap up soil to make it be raised, or do I need to have a structure around it?

ANSWER: That depends on how you water. Since I often water with the hose, I need a structure. If I were using only a slow watering method, like my oscillating sprinkler or a drip line (if you really must), then I think just heaping the filler would be fine. Make sure, however, that you still use a liner to block the weeds.

QUESTION: Can I put a cover on the raised bed and make it a mini greenhouse?

ANSWER: Yes, especially for spring, autumn, and winter.

QUESTION: We built some raised beds that are about three feet tall. We need to add more soil each year—it sinks down.

ANSWER: That wasn't really a question, but I'll take it. Your soil isn't really sinking—it's depleting. What I mean is that your soil is used up to create the vegetable plants. This is why it is important to compost—to give back to the earth the nutrients we take out. This avoids soil depletion. Add compost to your raised box to bring the soil level back up to height.

QUESTION: What is the strongest corner construction for untreated wood? The corners seem to go first.

ANSWER: I use a handsaw to cut pieces of four-by-four untreated lumber. But remember, you only need corner posts on tall frames. The most important thing you need to know about creating strong corners for raised garden boxes is to use screws, not nails, and to drill the holes for the screws before you insert the screws. If you don't drill holes first, you will crack the wood when you put the screws in, and the "life" of the corners will go down dramatically if the wood is cracked.

QUESTION: When are the times to use a box and when will I be okay with the good old-fashioned ground?

ANSWER: The ground is always going to be a victim of the weed seed bank. I use the good old-fashioned ground when I run out of box space, or when I want to do really large plantings, of wheat and corn for example. To make the most of the ground, use my edible weed killer recipe, as mentioned earlier in this chapter.

QUESTION: How do I keep field bindweed from coming up through my weed barrier?

ANSWER: Field bindweed (morning glory) is among that 5 percent that I was talking about when I said that raised bed gardening cuts out 95 percent of weeds. The good thing is that they are much easier to kill in boxes because the roots are so stringy. Spray with vinegar while they are young (five inches or less) and they will die—it may take a couple applications. Whatever you do, don't let them go to seed in your box.

QUESTION: Do I have to anchor the box?

ANSWER: No. If your box is wood, it is sufficiently heavy, and once it is filled, the soil anchors it. It might not be tornado proof, but what is?

QUESTION: How do I keep the box squared once I build it?

ANSWER: Build it short. As I said earlier, my long boxes have begun to bow out in the middle. Now I keep them short—eight feet long.

QUESTION: How much money does a box cost?

ANSWER: Let's add this up. Free wood, free liner, free filler. You might have to buy some screws, and you might have to buy a bit of organic compost. If you do, I'd say total cost per box would be about $3.50—three bucks for the compost, fifty cents for eight screws (I recommend two per corner). However, you can get screws for free by asking on Freecycle.org and among friends and neighbors. You might even be able to get free compost if you have not started making your own yet.

QUESTION: Are screws or nails best?

ANSWER: Screws. I use two-inch-long screws. I put

two on each corner, for a total of eight screws per raised bed box. I put one screw a third of the way down from the top, and one screw a third of the way up from the bottom. I pre-drill all eight holes before I put the screws in. This prevents the wood from cracking, which makes the corners much stronger, which makes the box last much longer.

QUESTION: Are the screws or nails going to rust? Will they hold if the box starts rotting?

ANSWER: If you buy the right screws, they will not rust. They need to be outdoor-rated screws. The wood will begin to rot over the course of years, but using two-inch-long screws put into pre-drilled holes without cracking the wood will make the boxes last at least twice as long. Untreated pine garden boxes in an arid climate could last as long as twenty years. In a humid climate they will go soft faster. Remember that my boxes are all doing great, and all of them were made with free wood that was old and weather worn to begin with. Some of my boxes are made from wood that had been sitting outside for two decades or more before it was given to me. When they do need to be replaced, it is cheap and easy—and you can usually lift the old box off without much trouble and build the new box right around the existing soil fill.

QUESTION: Can I move my frame after it has been in place a couple of years?

ANSWER: Yes, if you have two people lifting and carrying the empty frame so that you keep it level. If you don't keep it level, the screws will twist and pop out. If you are moving an aging box, you may need to install corner pieces to help strengthen it if you have stressed or popped out the screws.

I've moved several boxes and learned the hard way to get someone to help me so the box stays relatively level.

QUESTION: Should I use weed barrier and mulch on top of raised beds?

ANSWER: I suppose you could line the top with weed barrier, especially if you were putting in a permanent perennial herb garden, for example, but I don't think it's necessary. You could also use mulch or a new layer of compost on top each year. Try to keep the new layer just lower than the top of the box so that you don't wash it out of the box when you are watering.

QUESTION: Can I make a box out of cob?

ANSWER: A fascinating question, and I certainly would never have thought of it. Cob is a truly ancient technique for building homes, sheds, and other structures (even wood-fired ovens) out of a mix of clay, straw, water, and sand. Interest in cob construction has been surging over the past decade because cob is sustainable and potentially cheaper (although building codes in many places have not caught on yet and cob is still widely illegal, but change has already arrived in some places, and some modern cob homes have won awards).

But back to the question. The answer is no and yes. Normally, cob is quite thick—two feet thick, and obviously a two-foot-thick square of cob walls for a raised bed isn't going to be helpful, but because the cob walls for a raised bed garden would be quite low, I wonder how thin they could be. I've never built with cob. However, cob has amazing thermal mass, which is part of the reason it's been used for so long—it holds out heat in summer and retains it in winter. Which would make it ideal for building some kind of winter gardening box—potentially a three-sided, south-facing box with a south-facing slanted glass cover. I'm very intrigued by this idea and would not have thought of it without your question. I think I will try to build a cob winter garden cold frame this fall. It would be fun. I'll post updates about it on my blog at CalebWarnock.blogspot.com. And if you are experienced at cob building, email me and let's talk about you teaching a class for me. I'm at calebwarnock@yahoo.com.

QUESTION: Do I need to put a drain in the box?

ANSWER: Because your box is going to sit on a porous liner (newspaper) on the top of the raw earth, you do not need a drain. In fact, making the boxes shallow is partly to keep them from draining so much, which helps in arid climates. If you live in a humid rainy climate, the height of an eight- to twelve-inch-tall box will provide the drainage you need.

QUESTION: Any suggestions for a warmer climate like southern Utah? It's been a challenge learning to garden here. We have almost two growing seasons, with pauses in the winter and summer.

ANSWER: I get asked versions of this question a lot. Gardening in climates with summers in the 120s—and often mild winters—is a whole different ballgame. I have two suggestions. The first is to take full advantage of your mild winters with my book *Backyard Winter Gardening*—you could likely even grow cantaloupes and tomatoes in winter with just a simple cold frame, not even needing hotbeds. The second is to grow super–short season vegetables in spring and fall, when your climate is more amenable. In the heat of summer you could grow tomatoes with a layer of newspaper around them covered by a layer of mulch to help keep the water in the soil. The tomato plants won't produce in the blazing summer, but they will grow, and then when fall hits, they will be filled with tomatoes—which is exactly what happens in my geothermal greenhouse, which is 140 degrees most of the summer. Make sure you use only low raised beds, of course, to conserve as much water as possible. For short season vegetable seed, visit SeedRenaissance.com.

QUESTION: Eventually, the weeds do become a problem. Then what?

ANSWER: This is an interesting question. Here are a couple of reasons why weeds could become a problem over time in raised boxes, and what to do about it:

1. Weed seed blows in. This happens—dandelion, purslane, and bindweed seed are among the worst offenders because their seed is so light. Spot-spray with my edible weed killer recipe (SeedRenaissance.com). Don't let them go to seed in your box, which brings me to …

2. A few weeds got into your box and you were busy, and they went to seed, and then this happened a couple more years, and now your box looks like your regular garden soil—full of volunteer weeds. You could dig out the soil and start over with a new liner and new filler, which shouldn't be too hard, especially if you are using a shallow box. You could soak the soil in vinegar and solarize it for a couple of weeks by covering the entire box with a layer of plastic. This will work effectively to kill not only the weeds but often most of the weed seeds also, as

I mentioned earlier. Or use my edible weed killer recipe. Remember, raised bed boxes get rid of 95 percent of the weeds. It is up to us to make it a priority to spend a little time controlling those remaining 5 percent so they don't spread. Considering the alternative—and how little time it takes to control the 5 percent—it's worth making it a priority.

Finally, this question, posted by my friend, writers group member, and famous author of the internationally popular The Boleyn King series, Laura Andersen, who has recently abandoned us by moving to another state: "My question is: Will you come build one for me?"

ANSWER: Yes. Send two plane tickets and Charmayne and I are on our way.

Notes

1. Weathers, *French Market-Gardening*, 1.

2. Urban Homestead, "About the Urban Homestead City Farm."

3. Belliston, *Noxious Weed Field Guide to Utah*.

4. United States Environmental Protection Agency, "Preliminary Risk Assessment for Creosote."

CHAPTER 11
FULL-YEAR GARDEN CALENDAR

I've had many requests for a calendar spanning the full year to show when to plant which vegetables. As you use this calendar, please note that some vegetables can be planted over several months. Others, however, won't have time to mature if they are not planted as indicated.

JANUARY/FEBRUARY

The varieties listed for these two months are for planting from seed. I strongly suggest you do not start seeds indoors and transplant them to a hotbed because they will die of shock. This list assumes you have nightly or near-nightly below-freezing temperatures in winter months. If you are like me, your daytime temperatures may also rarely rise above freezing, especially in January. If you live in an area where night temperatures are consistently above freezing or mostly above freezing in January, you can use the March instructions in January. If your temperatures are tropical in January, please invite my wife and I to come and stay with you! I'll bring you some free books and seed! Meanwhile, you may skip to the June instructions, for use in January.

For the rest of us, I've chosen the following January and February varieties for the winter garden beginner. They are the easiest to sprout, and the most durable in bitter weather. A couple of quick notes on planting seed outdoors in January and February. You must at least have a cold frame made of greenhouse plastic (twin-wall polycarbonate) or glass. You must place the cold frame in the garden where you want to plant for at least a few days with sun before you plant so the sun can warm the soil. All snow has to be melted, and the ground has to be unfrozen (which is what the cold frame will do for you). Everything on the Jan./Feb. list will sprout faster and grow three times faster if you put it in a natural hotbed covered by a cold frame. Everything you need to know about hotbeds and cold frames is in my book *Backyard Winter Gardening*. Seeds for the special and often-rare winter varieties mentioned here are sold at SeedRenaissance.com.

- Cascadia peas in a hotbed, heated greenhouse, or geothermal greenhouse. These peas are almost unbelievably frost hardy—more hardy than all other peas I've tried. They germinate

A salad picked fresh in February in the author's winter garden. Winter gardening has seen a surge in interest since the author's *Backyard Winter Gardening* book was published.

The author checks a cold frame of lettuce in January.

in cold soil. Best of all, you can eat the leaves, which taste just like peas—just like them!—in salads, so you can start harvesting something immediately. Of course, don't overharvest the leaves or you won't get actual peas!

• Mizuna in a hotbed, heated greenhouse, or geothermal greenhouse. This extraordinary Asian green grows unbelievably fast. It does not seem at all fazed by bitter cold, and it has a beautiful frisee leaf. The goal of planting from seed in January is to get food self-sufficiently as fast as possible, which is why mizuna is a great choice. Do not confuse this with mizuna Golden Streaks, which is hot and not sweet.

• Rutabaga in a hotbed, heated greenhouse, or geothermal greenhouse. These wonderful root vegetables only sprout in cool weather, and right now they are thriving at my house, planted this month (January or February) from seed. These make the very best mashed potatoes. You probably haven't tried a rutabaga. They are like a cross between a carrot and a sugar beet in flavor. You'll love them! You can eat the young leaves in salads—great flavor.

• Vernal Red orach in a hotbed, heated greenhouse, or geothermal greenhouse. This is a relative of spinach, and you eat it just like spinach. It produces beautiful red-purple leaves that can be eaten raw or sautéed. I love it in an omelet or raw in salads! This vegetable just loves to sprout in winter. And it's great to have a fresh winter "green" that isn't green!

• Amsterdam Forcing carrots in a hotbed, heated greenhouse, or geothermal greenhouse. I have never been able to start carrots in January until I found this very old European winter carrot. I am one of only two sellers of this seed in the States.

• America spinach in a hotbed, heated greenhouse, or geothermal greenhouse. This is traditional spinach, and it will sprout in January, but it can be slow to grow, especially in the beginning. But once it is up and going, you'll have spinach all spring!

• Grand Rapids lettuce in a hotbed, heated greenhouse, or geothermal greenhouse . This is by far the fastest-growing lettuce out of more than one hundred varieties I have trialed—it is just amazing. If you want self-sufficient fresh lettuce fast, this is the place to start. In a hotbed it grows an astonishing four inches A WEEK! It is cut and comes again—so to harvest, just cut it off at the soil level. It will grow right back, over and over again.

• North Pole lettuce in a hotbed, heated greenhouse, or geothermal greenhouse. This unbelievable winter lettuce was developed by Fridtjof Nansen of Norway, who is famous for his pioneering exploration of the North Pole and winning the Nobel Peace Prize in 1922. I can't say enough about this lettuce, which has now become rare. It is also sold under the name *Arctic King*, and it was originally called *Nansen's Noordpool*. It has amazing cold-soil tolerance. It is a semi-romaine green lettuce with crisp, wonderful flavor. I'm proud to offer the seed for this true antique at SeedRenaissance.com.

• Extra dwarf pak choi in a hotbed, heated greenhouse, or geothermal greenhouse. A fun miniature Chinese cabbage that grows very fast and loves cold weather. Tender and succulent to eat, great steamed, raw, stir-fried, or in a salad!

• Osaka Purple mustard greens in a hotbed, heated greenhouse, or geothermal greenhouse. Purple and green leaves with a spicy kick. Put a little in a salad for a burst of flavor.

• Leeks in a heated greenhouse, a geothermal greenhouse, or indoors in a sunny window. Leaks need a long time to mature. If you do not plant leek seed by early March, you run the risk that they will not mature in your garden to a harvestable size in summer. I recommend American Flag leeks or Belgian Breeder's Winter Mix. But any leek will do.

• Blanc Hâtif de Paris onions can be planted in a hotbed in January and February for spring harvesting. They can also be planted in fall. I believe these to be the rarest onions in the world. For centuries they were the most popular onions for winter growing in Europe. I found out about them by reading some very old books, and I began a search for the seed. I couldn't find any anywhere, not even in Europe. I contacted the US National Plant Germplasm System, which serves as a sort of federal seed bank, and they did not have any, but they found some in a seed bank in the Netherlands and flew them over for me. I am now working to reintroduce these extremely valuable winter onions to the United States, where the seed has not been available for purchase for more than sixty years, according to my extensive research. These onions are nothing less than amazing winter performers. The seed is available only at SeedRenaissance.com.

• Globe onions can be planted from seed in January or February in a heated greenhouse, a geothermal greenhouse, or indoors in a sunny window. Onions come in three different types— short-day, intermediate-day, or long-day. What kind you need to plant depends entirely on your geography. Where I live, I have to plant long-day onions. If you are not sure which of the three types you need to plant, consult your local university extension service or ask a seasoned gardener in your area. To make matters more complicated, some globe onions are storage onions, meaning they will keep for months in a cold dark place. But some do not keep well at all, such as Walla Wallas. If your goal is self-sufficiency and you live in the West, I recommend Yellow Spanish globe onions. If you do not plant onion seed by early March, you run the risk that they will not have enough time to form a globe.

• Early Wonder and Early Wonder Tall Top beets are the best beets for planting in the greenhouse in January or February. These have been the beets with the best cold-soil tolerance in my tests.

• Red Iceberg lettuce sprouts amazingly well in hotbeds, especially in late January and February.

MARCH

• Broad Windsor fava beans can be planted from seed in the unprotected backyard garden just as soon as the ground can be worked. They will sprout within three weeks generally. To get them to sprout faster, plant this seed in a cold frame or cloche. To get them to flower in March, start them indoors in February and then transplant them into a cold frame or cloche in March, no sooner than the first week of March. Please note that Broad Windsor favas do not like hot weather. Where I live, by the end of June they have produced all their beans and then begin rapidly dying as the temperature rises. They can be planted until mid-April, and then I would consider it too late for them to develop—they shut down in the heat. They can be planted again in early autumn. These are pole beans but do not need any support. They typically produce three branches from the ground and flower very quickly, despite below-freezing nighttime temperatures. This variety is an amazing and very old English bean.

• Golden Sweet snow peas can be planted from seed in the unprotected backyard garden just as soon as the ground can be worked. They will sprout within three weeks generally. To get them to sprout faster, plant this seed in a cold frame or cloche. These are extremely fast to flower, second only to Tom Thumb peas, but they produce far more peas than Tom Thumbs. Also use the leaf tips and flowers in your salads for great fresh-pea flavor without the peas. These can also be planted in a greenhouse in March. When the peas are mature, they are exceptionally sweet. Big pods of big peas.

• Tom Thumb peas can be planted from seed in the unprotected backyard garden just as soon as the ground can be worked. They will sprout within three weeks generally. To get them to sprout faster, plant this seed in a cold frame or cloche. Out of about four dozen varieties of heirloom peas that I have trialed in my garden, these are the first to produce peas every time, in every trial. A truly amazing pea. These are very dwarf plants—the size of your hand when fully grown, and each plant generally produces about five pea pods These can also be planted in a greenhouse in March. You can even grow these in a sunny window in your house in pots in February and March. Because these are so dwarf, I do not recommend eating the leaf tips and flowers unless you are willing to risk not getting any peas.

• Cascadia peas can be planted from seed in the unprotected backyard garden just as soon as the

Fresh rutabaga harvested for Thanksgiving from the author's garden. Rutabaga is one of the least-used vegetables in the United States, with is unfortunate because it makes the best mashed "potatoes."

ground can be worked. They will sprout within three weeks generally. To get them to sprout faster, plant this seed in a cold frame or cloche. These peas are prolific and produce tons of peas. Cascadia peas have very waxy leaves, which make them the most winter hardy of all peas, but the wax also means these peas are not the best for harvesting the leafy tips for salads.

• Alaska peas produce peas a week earlier than Cascadia. These can be planted from seed in the unprotected backyard garden just as soon as the ground can be worked. They will sprout within three weeks generally. To get them to sprout faster, plant this seed in a cold frame or cloche. These peas are prolific and produce tons of peas. These are my favorite peas for eating the leafy tips and flowers. They have fantastic flavor.

• Tokyo bekana is a small Asian green with a sweet flavor that grows extremely fast. Great for salads. These can be planted from seed in the unprotected backyard garden just as soon as the ground can be worked. They will sprout within ten days generally, despite bitter temperatures. They will even sprout beneath snow. To get them to grow faster in bitter cold, plant this seed in a cold frame or cloche.

• Mizuna is an extraordinary Asian green, and it grows unbelievably fast. It does not seem at all fazed by bitter cold, and it has a beautiful frisee leaf. These can be planted from seed in the unprotected backyard garden just as soon as the ground can be worked. They will sprout within ten days generally, despite bitter temperatures. They will even sprout beneath snow. To get them to grow faster in bitter cold, plant this seed in a cold frame or cloche. Do not confuse this with mizuna Golden Streaks, which is spicy and not sweet.

A winter bean called Broad Windsor fava in bloom in the author's unheated geothermal greenhouse in March.

• Rutabaga in March can be planted in a cold frame, cloche, hotbed, or greenhouse. These wonderful root vegetables only sprout in cool weather, and right now they are thriving at my house, planted this month from seed. These make the best mashed potatoes. You probably haven't tried a rutabaga. They are like a cross between a carrot and a sugar beet in flavor. You'll love them! You can eat the young leaves in salads—great flavor. Rutabaga do not like heat and generally will not produce a bulb if planted later than March.

• Vernal Red orach shows off all its vernal power in March. Vernal is an astronomical term meaning that, if you vernalize this seed by planting it in the fall, it will spring happily up in a cold frame or cloche in late February or early March. In a cloche, I have harvestable leaves by the third week of March despite single-digit

temperatures! This will also sprout by mid-March in the unprotected backyard garden if the seed is planted in autumn. Interestingly, if you do not vernalize the seed, meaning if you just plant it in the backyard in March, it sprouts two to three weeks later than vernalized seed.

• Amsterdam Forcing carrots can be planted in March in a cold frame, cloche, hotbed, or greenhouse. These carrots spout faster than any other carrot I've ever tried. These are a traditional tapered orange carrot. They can be harvested as baby carrots within sixty days of sprouting generally.

• Parisienne carrots are shaped like a ball, not a taper. These carrots have been grown in winter in France for centuries using hotbeds. In March they can be planted in cold frames, cloches, hotbeds, or greenhouses.

• America spinach can be planted in March in a cold frame, cloche, hotbed, or greenhouse. You can even plant it in February and March in a pot in a sunny window in the house!

• Grand Rapids lettuce. This is by far the fastest growing lettuce out of more than one hundred varieties I have trialed—it is just amazing.

• Marvel of Four Seasons lettuce can be planted in March in a cold frame, cloche, hotbed, or greenhouse. This lettuce LOVES the cold frame in March and grows very fast. I love the flavor and bronzy-green color of this lettuce.

• Extra dwarf pak choi can be planted in March in a cold frame, cloche, hotbed, or greenhouse. This is a fun miniature Chinese cabbage that grows very fast and loves cold weather. It is tender and succulent to eat and great steamed, raw, stir-fried, or in salad!

- Osaka Purple mustard greens can be planted from seed in the unprotected backyard garden just as soon as the ground can be worked. They will sprout within twenty days generally, despite bitter temperatures. They will even sprout beneath snow. They will sprout and grow faster in bitter cold if planted in a cold frame or cloche. This plant has purple and green leaves with a spicy kick. Put a little in a salad for a burst of taste.

- French potimarron winter squash is amazingly tolerant of cold soil. In March, it can be planted in a cold frame or cloche and will generally sprout within two weeks.

- Costata Romanesco zucchini is stunningly tolerant of cold soil, much to my surprise. I have tested and retested this squash, and I still can't believe how well this old Italian heirloom produces in cold soil when planted in a cold frame or cloche. You can have summer squash before summer!

- Painted Lady scarlet runner beans are pole beans with the most beautiful orchid-like red flowers—and amazing cold-soil tolerance! These beans blew away the competition in my cold-soil tolerance trials. Plant in the backyard in March in a cold frame or cloche.

- Dragon Tongue bush beans are an old Scandinavian bean, which explains why they are so tolerant of cold soil. This is the only bush bean I have ever been able to get to thrive in cold soil! Plant in the backyard in March in a cold frame or cloche. These beans are not great for raw eating, but they are wonderful when blanched, steamed, or stir-fried. They are beautiful, with pods streaked in lime green and purple.

- Strawberry plants can be transplanted from runners in March or planted from seed in the open soil or started from seed in the house or greenhouse in January or February and then transplanted to a cloche or cold frame in March.

- Perennial herbs—including anise, hyssop, curry, horehound, thyme, lemon balm (also called Melissa), parsley, spearmint, peppermint, wintergreen, comfrey, catnip, echinacea (also called coneflower), rosemary, chamomile, oregano, or lavender (English or French)—can be planted from seed in March in cold frames, cloches, greenhouses, or indoors in a sunny window. When starting these indoors, transfer outdoors to a cold frame, cloche, or greenhouse as soon as the seeds sprout or the plants will become leggy and weak. Keep in mind that some herbs, like rosemary, are very slow to germinate. Keep them moist until they germinate.

- Potatoes can be planted outdoors in mid-March using the straw method (also called the French method, which is described in my first Forgotten Skills book) or in compost or in sandy or loamy garden soil.

- Noir des Carmes cantaloupe can be started in hotbeds in March. After lots of experience, take my word for it and put glue traps inside the hotbed frame in case you get voles or mice, which will eat your sprouts right to the ground.

- All beets can be planted in March in the open garden as soon as the soil can be worked, but they will sprout and grow faster in a cold frame or cloche. Early Wonder and Early Wonder Tall Top have been the beets with the best cold-soil tolerance in my garden tests.

- Tomatoes can be started from seed (only from seed—transplants will die of shock) in

March hotbeds. For instructions on building a natural-heat hotbed, see my book *Backyard Winter Gardening*. Only a few varieties will work in hotbeds in March, and they all originated in Siberia. They are Moskvich, Sub-Arctic Plenty, and Snow Fairy, and they are available at SeedRenaissance.com.

• Mammoth Melting peas are huge, sweet peas with edible pods that are a winner of my cold-soil tolerance tests. They can be planted in the open garden in March. These plants produce remarkably big peas, but not as many peas as Cascadia.

• Swiss chard can be planted in cold frames or cloches in March.

• North Pole lettuce. This unbelievable winter lettuce was developed by Fridtjof Nansen of Norway, who is famous for his pioneering exploration of the North Pole and winning the Nobel Peace Prize in 1922 for his work to stop starvation in Europe after World War I. I can't say enough about this lettuce, which has now become rare. It is also sold under the name Arctic King, and it was originally called Nansen's Noordpool. It has amazing cold soil tolerance. It is a semi-romaine green lettuce with crisp, wonderful flavor. I'm proud to offer the seed for this true antique at SeedRenaissance.com.

APRIL

PLEASE NOTE: These instructions for April are based on gardens that experience below-freezing temperatures in April. If your garden does not experience any below-freezing temperatures in April, you can follow the May instructions beginning in April.

• All fava beans should be planted no later than mid-April for best results. Broad Windsor fava beans can be planted from seed until mid-April, but I live at five thousand feet—the higher your elevation, the shorter your growing season. If your April does not have below-freezing night temperatures, it is too late for you to plant favas.

• All peas can be planted in the open garden in April.

• All Asian greens can be planted in the open garden in April.

• Vernal Red orach can be planted in the open garden in April.

• All carrots can be planted in the open garden in April.

• All spinach can be planted in the open garden in the last half of April.

• French potimarron winter squash is amazingly tolerant of cold soil. It can be planted in a cold frame or cloche in April and will generally sprout within a week.

• Costata Romanesco zucchini is stunningly tolerant of cold soil when planted in a cold frame or cloche in April.

• All so-called runner beans can be planted in cold frames or cloches in April.

• Dragon Tongue bush beans can be planted in cold frames or cloches in April.

• Strawberries can be transplanted from runners in April or started from seed.

• All perennial herbs can be planted in the open garden in April, either as transplants or from seed.

• All potatoes can be planted outdoors in April.

• Noir des Carmes cantaloupe can be started in hotbeds in April.

- All beets can be planted in the open garden in April.

- For planting tomatoes in April, follow the March directions.

- Swiss chard can be planted in the open ground in April.

- All lettuces can be planted in the open garden in April.

MAY

Everything except heat-intolerant plants like fava beans, runner beans, and rutabagas can be planted in the open garden in May if your last average frost date has passed. Until your last average frost date has passed (which for me is May 15-ish), continue to use the April schedule in May.

JUNE

Everything except heat-intolerant plants like fava beans, runner beans, and rutabagas can be planted in the open garden if your last average frost date has passed, which it has in June for the vast majority of the contiguous United States. However, in the last half of June it will begin to be too late to plant vegetables with a long day count. The day count is the number of days it takes a plant to produce a vegetable. The count begins on the day the plant opens its second set of leaves, also called true leaves. Tomatoes, for example, come in an enormous array of day counts, ranging from two hundred days at the long end to forty days at the short end. In short season areas like mine, at five thousand feet elevation, I have no choice but to plant only short season vegetables. For the best, most vigorous, and most reliable short season vegetable varieties, see SeedRenaissance.com.

Heirloom carrots in all colors of the rainbow harvested in August in the author's garden.

JULY

Follow the June instructions regarding short season vegetables. The last week of July also marks the beginning of the fall garden planting season. The fall vegetables with the longest day counts will need to be planted in the last week of July and no later than the second week of August. These include autumn beans, most peas, rutabagas, and cabbages.

AUGUST

All fall and winter vegetables can be planted in August. These include:

- Cascadia peas

- Mizuna

- Rutabaga

- Vernal Rose orach

- Parisienne carrots
- America spinach
- Grand Rapids lettuce
- Extra dwarf pak choi
- Osaka Purple mustard greens
- All leeks (for spring harvesting)
- All garlic (for spring harvesting)
- Blanc Hâtif de Paris onions (for spring harvesting)
- Early Wonder and Early Wonder Tall Top beets
- Broad Windsor fava beans
- Golden Sweet snow peas
- Tom Thumb peas
- Alaska peas
- Tokyo bekana

- Marvel of Four Seasons lettuce
- Dragon Tongue bush beans
- Perennial herbs, can be divided and transplanted but not started from seed
- Mammoth melting peas
- Swiss chard
- North Pole lettuce

SEPTEMBER

The following fall and winter vegetables can be planted from seed in the open garden in September:

- Mizuna
- Rutabaga
- Vernal Rose orach
- Parisienne carrots
- America spinach
- Grand Rapids lettuce
- Extra dwarf pak choi
- Osaka Purple mustard greens
- All leeks (for spring harvesting)
- All garlic (for spring harvesting)
- Blanc Hâtif de Paris onions (for spring harvesting)
- Early Wonder and Early Wonder Tall Top beets
- Broad Windsor fava beans, in early September only
- Golden Sweet snow peas
- Tom Thumb peas
- Alaska peas for pea greens (they will only produce peas now if you have a late winter)

A stand of corn is overlooked by the mountains in the author's summer garden.

- Tokyo bekana
- Marvel of Four Seasons lettuce
- Perennial herbs, can be divided and transplanted but not started from seed
- Swiss chard
- North Pole lettuce

OCTOBER

I cover all fall and winter vegetables with cloches or cold frames around Halloween when regular heavy frosts (28 degrees or below for more than two hours) set in. You should cover your garden for the winter depending on when your regular heavy frosts set in, including any fall or winter vegetables planted in July, August, September, or this month.

The following can be planted from seed in the open garden in October and can be left uncovered for lights frosts (29–32 degrees):

- Mizuna
- Vernal Rose orach
- America spinach
- Grand Rapids lettuce
- Extra dwarf pak choi
- Osaka Purple mustard greens
- All leeks (for spring harvesting)
- All garlic (for spring harvesting)
- Blanc Hâtif de Paris onions (for spring harvesting)
- Alaska peas (for pea greens only)
- Tokyo bekana
- Marvel of Four Seasons lettuce

- Perennial herbs, can be divided and transplanted but not started from seed.
- Swiss chard
- North Pole lettuce

Some mature summer vegetables (planted in spring) and some perennial herbs will need to be covered in cloches or cold frames by the end of October if you want them to continue to produce through winter; they include:

- Swiss chard
- Collard greens
- Lemon balm
- Parsley
- Thyme
- Rosemary

The following mature herbs and perennial vegetables need no covering all winter to survive (they will not, however, produce a harvest):

- Mint herbs
- Common chives
- Garlic chives
- Egyptian walking onions
- Sunchokes (also called Jerusalem artichokes)
- Strawberries
- Berry bushes
- Mature carrots can be covered with a low cold frame, but they might not last the winter. They will be best if covered in October according to the directions in my book *Backyard Winter Gardening*.

- Mature Danish Ballhead cabbages can continue to be harvested all winter without being covered. There will be some frost damage on the outer leaves, which should be peeled off and composted or given to the chickens. Cabbages harvested frozen should be used fresh or cooked before they reach room temperature, after which they will begin to die.

- Winter Green Jewel romaine lettuce that is planted in autumn will produce all winter without any covering, but it will produce more and faster under a cold frame.

NOVEMBER

Vegetables in cloches or cold frames will remain covered until March except for harvesting and occasional watering (see details in *Backyard Winter Gardening*, which also has complete information on hotbeds). The following can be planted from seed in hotbeds in November:

- Mizuna
- Vernal Rose orach
- America spinach
- Extra dwarf pak choi
- Osaka Purple mustard greens
- Tokyo bekana
- Swiss chard

- Winter lettuces , as found at SeedRenaissance.com
- Blanc Hâtif de Paris onions

DECEMBER

Vegetables in cloches or cold frames will remain covered until March except for harvesting and occasional watering (see details in my book *Backyard Winter Gardening*, which also has complete information on hotbeds). The following can be planted from seed in hotbeds in December:

- Mizuna
- Vernal Rose orach
- Osaka Purple mustard greens
- Tokyo bekana
- Swiss chard
- Winter lettuces, as found at SeedRenaissance.com
- Blanc Hâtif de Paris onions
(for spring harvesting)

You may wonder why the list of things that can be planted in hotbeds in January is much larger than the list that can be planted in December. The answer has to do with how winter vegetables rely on the cues of the astronomical winter solstice in late December. For a full explanation, see *Backyard Winter Gardening*.

CHAPTER 12
PERENNIAL COLOR PARADE:
CREATING A SUMMERLONG SUCCESSION OF BLOOMS

If you want lots of colorful flowers for the whole summer season, with little to no work, perennials are your answer! At our house, we rely on perennials. My wife plants a few annual petunias if she gets around to it, and I try to remember to start some marigolds and zinnias in the greenhouse, but to be frank, some years I don't get around to it. This year is one of those years.

Thank goodness for perennials. We've put tons of perennial flowers into our yard because they are drought tolerant, and they come up every year without any help from us. Perennials are the landscaping answer for every busy family. Planting a perennial succession bed, stocked with flowers that will provide a succession of blooms beginning in spring and lasting through fall, is an easy color guarantee. Below is a list of perennial flowers arranged according to their blooming schedule, to take all the guesswork out of creating a succession perennial bed. I have also created a couple of color-themed sample gardens that will provide constant color from spring through autumn. Or use the list to design your own—just pick your favorites, making sure you have a handful of plants that will be in bloom at any one time, according to the chart.

In putting this list together, I poured over years of photographs of my garden (which luckily I file by date), rather than trying to rely on my memory. This is certainly not a comprehensive list, but these are the perennials we enjoy year after year. Orach and cosmos are not actually perennials, but they self-seed so reliably that it doesn't matter. Orach could spread if you don't pull up any extra plants. Orach and hosta are ornamental, grown for their foliage not their flowers, although hostas do produce beautiful July flowers. A few of the plants on this list are marked as reblooming, which means they will bloom twice—once early in the season and then again late in the season. These include mountain geranium, dianthus, calla lilies, and Blue & Gold tradescantia. Perennials are far cheaper when started from seed. You can find seed for perennial flowers at SeedRenaissance.com.

EARLY-APRIL BLOOMING

- Daffodils

- Vernal Red orach
(ornamental and edible for purple foliage)

LATE-APRIL BLOOMING

- Bleeding hearts

- Daffodils

- Grape hyacinth (muscari)

- Tulips

- Vernal Red orach
(ornamental and edible for purple foliage)

EARLY-MAY BLOOMING

- Bleeding hearts

- Daffodils

Dame's rocket

Mums

- Grape hyacinth (muscari)

- Hosta (ornamental)

- Tulips

- Vernal Red orach
(ornamental and edible for purple foliage)

LATE-MAY BLOOMING

- Allium

- Buttercups

- Chives

- Grape hyacinth (muscari)

- Hosta (ornamental)

- Poppies

- Tulips

- Vernal Red orach
(ornamental and edible for purple foliage)

- Wild roses

EARLY-JUNE BLOOMING

- Blue & Gold tradescantia

- Buttercups

- Columbines

- Dame's rocket

- Dianthus

- Grape hyacinth (*muscari*)

- Hosta (ornamental)

- Mountain geranium

- Peonies

- Primrose

- Salvia

Wild roses

Daisies

Snapdragons

- Snapdragons
- Tulips
- Vernal Red orach
(ornamental and edible for purple foliage)
- Wild roses

LATE-JUNE BLOOMING

- Blackberries
- Buttercups
- Butterfly weed
- Catmint
- Columbines
- Curry
- Daisies
- Dame's rocket
- Daylilies

Primrose

- Dianthus
- Hollyhocks
- Horehound
- Hosta (ornamental)
- Lavender
- Mountain geranium
- Primrose
- Red clover
- Roses
- Salvia
- Snapdragons
- Sweet peas
- Yarrow

EARLY-JULY BLOOMING

- Black-eyed Susans

- Butterfly bush
- Butterfly weed
- Calla lilies
- Canterbury bells
- Catmint
- Coneflowers
- Curry
- Daisies
- Daylilies
- Dianthus
- Easter lilies
- Gaillardia Indian Blanket
- Hollyhocks
- Horehound
- Hosta (ornamental and flowers in July)
- Lavender
- Primrose
- Roses
- Salvia
- Snapdragons
- Sweet Peas
- Yarrow

- Catmint
- Coneflowers
- Cosmos
- Curry
- Daylilies
- Easter lilies
- Gaillardia Indian Blanket
- Horehound
- Hosta (ornamental and flowers in July)
- Lavender
- Primrose
- Roses
- Russian sage

LATE-JULY BLOOMING

- Black-eyed Susans
- Butterfly bush
- Butterfly weed
- Calla lilies
- Canterbury bells

Mountain geraniums

- Salvia
- Snapdragons
- Sunflowers
- Sweet Peas
- Yarrow

EARLY-AUGUST BLOOMING

- Black-eyed Susans
- Butterfly weed
- Canterbury bells
- Chrysanthemums
- Coneflowers
- Cosmos

Easter lilies and coneflowers

- Daylilies
- Dianthus (reblooming)
- Gaillardia Indian Blanket
- Hibiscus bush
- Horehound
- Hosta (ornamental)
- Lavender
- Oregano
- Primrose
- Roses
- Russian sage
- Salvia
- Snapdragons
- Sunflowers
- Sweet Peas
- Yarrow

LATE-AUGUST BLOOMING

- Black-eyed Susans
- Chrysanthemums
- Coneflowers
- Cosmos
- Daylilies
- Dianthus (reblooming)
- Gaillardia Indian Blanket
- Hibiscus bush
- Hosta (ornamental)
- Mountain geraniums (reblooming)
- Oregano

- Primrose
- Roses
- Russian sage
- Snapdragons
- Sunflowers

EARLY-SEPTEMBER BLOOMING

- Chrysanthemums
- Snapdragons
- Salvia
- Sunflowers
- Coneflowers
- Gaillardia Indian Blanket
- Butterfly bush
- Russian sage
- Calla lilies (reblooming)

LATE-SEPTEMBER BLOOMING

- Chrysanthemums
- Russian sage
- Salvia

EARLY-OCTOBER BLOOMING

- Blue & Gold tradescantia (reblooming)
- Chrysanthemums
- Russian sage
- Salvia

Tradescantia

LATE-OCTOBER BLOOMING

- Chrysanthemums

SAMPLE GARDENS

The sample gardens below are based on color theme, provide a succession of flowers from spring through autumn, are all perennial flowers, and are labeled according to height so you know whether to place them in the front of the flower bed (short flowers), the middle, or the back (tall flowers).

Sample Succession Garden in Cool Hues (Blue, Purple, Green, White)

- (Short) Grape hyacinth (late April through early May)
- (Short) Primrose (June through autumn)
- (Short) Tulips (late April through early June)

- **(Short, medium)** Dianthus (June through autumn)
- **(Short, medium)** Hosta (ornamental spring through fall)
- **(Short, medium)** Snapdragons (June through autumn)
- **(Medium)** Canterbury bells (July)
- **(Medium)** Chrysanthemums (early August through late October)
- **(Medium)** Columbines (June)
- **(Medium)** Daylilies (late June through autumn)
- **(Medium)** Oregano (July and August)
- **(Medium)** Salvia (June through autumn)
- **(Medium to tall)** Coneflowers (early July through late August)
- **(Tall)** Daisies (late June and July)
- **(Tall)** Dame's rocket (June)
- **(Tall)** Roses (June through autumn)

- **(Tall)** Russian sage (late July through autumn)
- **(Tall)** Vernal Red orach (ornamental early April through July)

Sample Succession Garden in Warm Hues (Yellow, Orange, Red, White)

- **(Short)** Daffodils (blooming early April through early May)
- **(Short)** Dianthus (June through autumn)
- **(Short)** Gaillardia Indian Blanket (early July through late August)
- **(Short)** Pink muscari (late April through early May)
- **(Short)** Primrose (June through autumn)
- **(Short)** Tulips (late April through early June)
- **(Short, medium)** Bleeding hearts (late April through early May)
- **(Short, medium)** Chrysanthemums (early August through late October)

- **(Short, medium)** Hosta (ornamental spring through fall)
- **(Short, medium)** Snapdragons (June through autumn)
- **(Medium)** Columbines (June)
- **(Medium)** Daylilies (late June through autumn)
- **(Medium)** Poppies (late May)
- **(Tall)** Daisies (late June and July)
- **(Tall)** Roses (June through autumn)
- **(Tall)** Yarrow (June through autumn)

CHAPTER 13

WILD EDIBLE VEGETABLES

I admit that it was visitors touring my garden who first brought me around to the full possibilities of wild vegetables. My only regret is that I didn't catch on sooner.

My first Forgotten Skills book has my recipe for dandelion ravioli and a history of how the pilgrims brought dandelions to this country as a "hunger gap" food for both humans and honeybees. After reading my first book, my neighbor became intensely interested in wild vegetables. And she was the one who eventually converted me. My wife and I eat something from our property almost every day, and having entire meals from our property is not unusual. In 2012, we had our first salad for dinner that was entirely made of wild or self-producing vegetables—a first for us. What was in it?

- the first purslane of the year
- tender tips of wild spinach (lambsquarters)
- dandelion leaves
- mallow leaves
- mallow peas
- self-seeding buttercrunch lettuce
- self-seeding Osaka Purple mustard greens

- perennial purple chive flowers

I was teaching a class recently about "giving yourself a raise" by lowering your food bill by eating out of your garden year-round. There was a man in the audience who interrupted me to say he was an accountant and there was an aspect of saving money I hadn't mentioned: sales tax. In Utah, where I live, every time I get something out of my garden, not only have I saved gas to go to the store and back and the cost of the food, but I've also saved by avoiding sales tax. That money can go to more important uses—getting a family out of debt, going to a worthy charity, or saving toward a great family vacation. There is no easier way to give yourself a raise than to have a wild vegetable salad for lunch. And you'll be surprised at the great taste.

Before we go over the wild edibles one at a time, here are some "rules" for wildcrafting your food.

1. If you collect wild vegetables, make sure you are getting the right plants. This is not too difficult, but learning to correctly identify wild plants takes a bit of practice. Be sure you know what you are putting in your mouth. Don't hesitate to ask for help in online gardening forums, and look in your area for someone who already eats wild vegetables (there

Baby purslane

Purslane flower

are a lot more of us than you might think, even in cities) and who might be willing to take you on a "wild garden walk" to show you the ropes. I have included photos in this chapter for your convenience, and there are also books on the market that specialize in this subject. This chapter deals with the wild vegetables that grow where I live that we eat a lot of, but you are likely to have wild vegetables in your state that we don't have, so finding like-minded people with experience in your own area can't hurt. I also teach edible wild vegetable classes with recipes (backyard chocolate mousse, anyone?) both online and in person. You can get details by emailing me at calebwarnock@yahoo.com.

A list of free online sources for edible wild plant information that I trust:

- Plants.usda.gov—this is the plants database of the United States Department of Agriculture.

This site offers a great search engine, many useful photos, and a lot of other useful information.

- Pfaf.org/user/edibleuses.aspx—This is the edible plants section on the Plants for a Future website, which includes detailed descriptions with photos. This website is invaluable.

- Loc.gov/rr/scitech/tracer-bullets/edibleplantstb.html—This is the Library of Congress edible wild plants bulletin, which will guide you to an enormous amount of fascinating information—I am especially intrigued by the collection of old edible wild plants cookbooks. I recommend going straight to the "Selected Internet Resources" section here: http://www.loc.gov/rr/scitech/tracer-bullets/edibleplantstb.html.

- Wildmanstevebrill.com—This great website will give you tons of great photos of wild edibles and even recipes. Best of all, Steve Brill has released several apps for wild foraging that you can download. Even the Library of Congress recommends him!

You can also find websites about edible wild plants specific to every state, often sponsored by a local university. Doing a google search for edible wild plants with the name of your state should bring that up for you.

2. Whether collecting in your yard or elsewhere, only gather wild food that you know has not been sprayed with chemicals. And make sure that you have permission to gather if you are taking food from land that is not your own.

3. Don't strip Mother Nature's garden. Never take more than a quarter of the total population of a wild vegetable in any given small area. Remember that these plants naturally self-seed, so if you "strip mine" a whole section of land, you've ruined your future eating opportunities. Take only what you will eat without wasting, and never take more than half of what is available in one spot in one year. Or better yet . . .

4. "Herd" wild vegetables into your garden and encourage them to establish themselves there. Although all the wild vegetables in this chapter grow in many places on our property, I have encouraged them to establish in my garden space, where I know they won't be trampled by the little kids (or unwitting adults), the dogs, or the pasture animals or chickens. I don't want to be serving fresh wild edibles for lunch or supper that have been walked on or dirtied by our animals.

5. If you are nervous about your ability to identify or find wild vegetables, you can always grow them from seed in your own garden. This will give you a chance to observe what the plants look like at all stages of growth without having to worry about whether you have identified the plant correctly—and once your garden patch is established, it will seed itself from then on. For seeds for edible wild vegetables and backyard wild medicinal herbs, visit SeedRenaissance.com.

Purslane (*Portulaca oleracea*)

Purslane grows as a "weed" in our yard, but it is a popular vegetable in the Mediterranean. The wonderful book *Edible Wild Plants* by John Kallas says that purslane has more than twice as much omega-3 as kale, huge amounts of vitamin E, and as much iron as spinach.[1] And the taste: perfection. Sweet, lightly crunchy, delicious.

Where I live, purslane erupts out of the ground in June as an odd-looking purple acne of sorts, but it grows quickly, and as it grows, it turns green. Purslane likes to creep out along the ground rather than grow up into the air, and sometimes a single plant can get up to two feet across. Don't wait until the plants are huge, however, to start eating them because the older they get, the less tasty they are. I start harvesting as soon as the purslane is big enough to bother with—a couple of inches across. When the plant gets much larger than six inches, you'll want to start harvesting the tender ends of the vines rather than the whole plant. Wildmanstevebrill.com has recipes for purslane salad and purslane potato salad.

Wild Spinach (*Chenopodium album*)

Lambsquarter is a genetic relative of spinach, and John Kallas suggests that real food enthusiasts should call this wild spinach because that is really what it is. We eat the tips, which are the most dense and tender. Kallas says it has more fiber and vitamins A and C than garden spinach, along with a list of other benefits.[2] Taste is like a mild spinach.

Dandy noodles

Wild spinach begins growing in my geothermal greenhouse in late February, but outside in the garden it does not sprout until June. This is probably the single wild vegetable that we eat the most of because the plants are prolific and thrive, growing up to three feet tall. We use this as a salad, but wildmanstevebrill.com has a recipe for lambsquarter spread.

Dandelions (*Taraxacum officinale*)

Dandelion leaves should be eaten, not poisoned! Why waste this healthy, flavorful free food? For the full story of dandelions as food, see my first Forgotten Skills book. Dandelions—which to this day are sold in Italian grocery stores instead of lettuce—are far more nutritious than any lettuce you can grow or buy. And if you know how to prepare them, they are never bitter.

According to wildmanstevebrill.com, dandelion leaves have more beta-carotene than carrots. He calls the iron and calcium content "phenomenal, greater than spinach" and says they are rich in B vitamins and a bunch of other nutrients too.[3] But the most important thing he has to say about them, to me, is this: "People today shun bitter flavors, they're so conditioned by overly sweet or salty processed food. But in earlier times, we distinguished between good and bad bitterness. Mixed with other flavors, as in a salad, dandelions improve the flavor."[4]

There is a wonderful new cookbook by Kristina Seleshanko called *The Ultimate Dandelion Cookbook*, which has my favorite dandelion recipe (besides my ravioli)—Dandelion Noodles. Making green pasta with dandelions is quick and easy.

Common Mallow (*Malva neglecta*)

When my neighbor asked me if she could transplant a mallow weed from my garden to hers, I was gobsmacked. I hate mallow. The roots must go ten feet deep. My neighbor convinced me to eat them, not fight them. Sweet revenge! You might remember this plant from childhood as the "cheese" plant when you popped mallow peas in your mouth. This plant is also called dwarf mallow. This is not the same plant as marsh mallow (*Althaea officinalis*, also called *Malva officinalis*), which is much harder to find in the United States but is also edible.

We eat the leaves of common mallow in salads in spring, summer, and fall, and if you put them in cheesecloth or a tea ball, you can boil them in soup to use as a thickener and then remove them. My favorite part of this plant are the peas, which look like little round green buttons. These you eat as peas, and they make marshmallows—yes, marshmallows!

Here are some recipes:

Mallow Peas

Step 1. Pick a handful of these peas. Some people try to remove the pods, but that is a waste of time and nutrition.

Step 2. Wash the peas and then barely cover them with water in a small saucepan. Boil them until only half the water remains. Drain and serve warm, but don't throw out the water, because you will use it to make marshmallows.

BACKYARD MARSHMALLOWS

- ¼ cup thick water drained from boiling mallow peas

- 1 egg white

- ¼ cup sugar

- ¼ teaspoon cream of tartar (optional)

Step 1. Let the drained liquid cool completely. In a bowl, use an electric beater to whip liquid until it begins to resemble soft meringue.

Mallow leaves

Mallow peas

Step 2. Add egg white, sugar, and cream of tartar (optional). Whip with the beater until the white foam forms hard peaks.

Step 3. Use a spoon to place large marshmallow-shaped dollops of foam on a cookie sheet. Bake marshmallows for 15–20 minutes on 300 degrees, or until they begin to brown. Cool and serve!

RECIPE VARIATIONS: You can also use this recipe to make meringue for pies. If you are artistic and careful, you can bake your own marshmallow Peeps candy by forming the raw foam into rabbit shapes. You could even add a drop of food coloring to color them.

Cattail (*Typha latifolia* and *Typha augustifolia*)

The pioneers who settled the West used to grind cattail fluff to extend flour in times of hunger. I have not tried this myself. There is also a use of cattail that everyone should know about—a firestarter. Everyone should have a bag of dried cattail fluff in their camping gear and their emergency gear, because when it comes to lighting fires, there is nothing else like it in the world. If you put a match to a handful of dried cattail fluff, it practically explodes into flame. Try it sometime—it's fascinating to watch, and it makes starting campfires so easy. We are lucky because

cattails planted themselves in our homemade backyard pond, so we have our own supply, but cattails grow wild most anywhere there is water, at least where I live.

Others

Shepherd's purse, chickweed, burdock, clover, common plantain, daylilies—these are just a few of the others we have on our property that we use occasionally, but I find them to be less useful for everyday eating, usually because the window of opportunity is shorter or they produce such small quantities. If you are interested in learning more about these, wildmanstevebrill.com is a great place to start. The other ingredients to the salad listed at the beginning of this chapter—buttercrunch lettuce, Osaka Purple mustard greens, and purple chive flowers—will be covered in the next chapter of this book because they are only "wild" in the sense that you don't have to do any work to grow them once they are established.

Notes

1. Kallas, *Edible Wild Plants*, 130.

2. Ibid., 68.

3. Brill, "Common Dandelion (*Taraxacum Officinale*)."

4. Ibid.

CHAPTER 14

THE EASIEST GARDEN YOU'LL EVER GROW:

SELF-SEEDING VEGETABLES

I'm always happy when vegetables in my garden plant themselves. There is no easier gardening in the world!

Some vegetable varieties are simply more willing to self-plant than others. Over the years, I've taken note of my best volunteers so I can recruit them year after year. After all, if there is a vegetable that wants to plant itself, I'm too busy to argue and only too grateful to have the help.

At the time of this writing, self-planted vegetables that have come up this fall include mustard greens, cabbages, rutabaga, peas, lettuce, and beans. In October, I even found a baby tomato plant, about an inch high. All of my other outdoor tomatoes have frozen, but this one is fine and happy because it is so close to the ground, it didn't get frozen (the ground releases heat at night). So I put a cloche over it, and so far it's doing great! We'll see what happens.

Another great thing about self-planted veggies is that they thrive. For example, I planted some

rutabagas, but the rutabagas that planted themselves came up before anything I planted, and are now more advanced and will produce mature roots before the ones I planted. Kinda makes me wonder why I even bothered planting.

One caveat of self-planted volunteers is that you may not want them where they are growing. I had beans volunteer, but where I have them is covered by a low cold frame for winter lettuces. The beans were crowding the lettuce and needed more space. So I transplanted the beans over to the beans I planted in fall—and they are all thriving in full flower right now.

When I married my wife, she told me the rule of the house was that everyone and everything has to thrive on benign neglect, including husbands. In the garden, this means that the vegetables have to do most of the work themselves—we are busy. So when the garden plants itself, it's just following the rules.

Speaking of rules, here are some quick rules for helping your self-planted vegetables thrive:

Marvel of Four Seasons lettuce

1. To self-seed, the plant must produce seed. If you eat everything from the plant, these vegetables can't do their self-seeding work, so make sure you leave some behind.

2. Don't till your soil. I practice no-till gardening, and a self-seeding garden is just one of the many side benefits of not disturbing the soil. If you till, seeds can't plant themselves.

3. Don't spray or use preemergent herbicides. Our garden is organic, so this is not a problem for us.

4. Be willing to share your pathways. Self-seeders often plant themselves in garden pathways. If they have planted enough of themselves in your regular garden beds, you could simply pull them out of your pathways, but I always find this hard to do no matter how many I have—I have a hard time getting rid of perfectly good free food. So I share my pathways. If space gets really tight, I pull up just enough plants to get through.

5. Prevent cross-pollination. For the lettuces, beans, and tomatoes listed in this chapter, this is not really a problem for reasons that are outside the scope of this book, but Asian greens, for example, are notorious for promiscuous cross-pollination. If you have more than one variety flowering at a time, your self-seeding crossers will change over time and are likely to slowly die out.

6. Be sure to water. Just because the vegetables are self-planted doesn't mean they don't need water in summer if you live in a dry climate like I do. In spring, when the plants are young, they usually don't need any additional watering.

7. Don't let the self-planted vegetables run amok. This is the most important rule of keeping a self-seeding garden—keep them on your property. Of all the plants I discuss in this chapter, Vernal Red orach is the mostly likely to spread beyond the borders of your garden and into the wild if you let it. Don't let it. Fortunately, because of its distinctive leaf shape and bright purple color, this plant is easy to recognize even when it is young, so if you think it's getting out of control, pull up the offending plants.

Here is a list of the best self-planting vegetable varieties (all of these are available at SeedRenaissance.com):

VERNAL RED ORACH

This beautiful vegetable is one of my all-time favorites. It is popular in Europe but little known here. I'm on a one-man crusade to popularize this vegetable in North America. Beyond all of its other virtues (color, taste, nutrition, cold-hardiness), it is one of the single best self-seeders I've ever encountered.

BUTTERCRUNCH LETTUCE

This is a green, sweet, crisp looseleaf lettuce that loves to self-seed. Just make sure you keep an eye on it in the spring so that you don't mistake it for an early weed and pull it out! In my garden, this lettuce comes back year after year if grown on ground I don't till. It is not a true perennial, but it self-seeds extremely reliably if you let a few heads go to seed. This is dwarf sized, with green leaves, and it grows fast. It works well for fresh winter garden growing as well as summer.

GABRIELLA LETTUCE

This lovely burgundy lettuce comes back with good reliability, and I'm always startled to find it growing in my garden pathways and beds with its striking color. Great flavor too. This lettuce is almost impossible to find, and I am proud to offer it at SeedRenaissance.com.

MARVEL OF FOUR SEASONS LETTUCE

There is a reason this lettuce has been a garden favorite for more than five hundred years—yes, you read that right! With the correct conditions, this determined lettuce self-seeds like clockwork. It is a favorite of ours because of its stunning color—red/bronze/green with touches of purple. (In cold weather, it is mostly purple). The lettuce also has a better taste than most lettuces—and best of all, it grows well during all four seasons, including in a cold frame in winter.

EXTRA DWARF PAK CHOI

This super–fast growing little Chinese looseleaf cabbage is succulent and in demand since being featured in my first book. It will self-seed in your garden in both spring and fall. I've actually had this Asian green go to flower in my garden on December 5! Great for fresh eating or steaming.

INDIAN WOMAN YELLOW BUSH BEANS

A self-seeding bean is unusual, so you can imagine how caught off guard I was when I discovered its self-perpetuating tendencies. It doesn't self-seed thickly, but it reliably produces at least as many new plants as the number of plants the seed came from, if not more, which is pretty staggering for a bean plant. This bean is also super early and hard to find. In fact, last time I checked, my seed site, SeedRenaissance .com, was the only place to offer this seed for sale.

Pak choi

Mountain Rose potatoes

OSAKA PURPLE MUSTARD GREENS

This has a dark purple color—the colder it is, the more purple it is—and a prolific plant. The flavor is spicy when it is eaten raw, and I've had some people compare the flavor to horseradish. The heat almost totally disappears when sautéed or steamed. It stays fresh though January or longer in a cold frame, and it works well for fresh winter garden growing as well as summer.

NOIR DES CARMES CANTALOUPES

This is a remarkable melon for so many reasons, not the least of which is its uncanny ability to self-seed. In fact, it self-seeds in my garden every year. I've been studying this melon for several years, and there is mounting evidence that it is self-pollinating, which may contribute to its unusual tendency to self-seed.

This is both a winter and summer cantaloupe, traditionally grown in hotbeds starting in January. I have also sprouted this melon in the first week of February in my geothermal greenhouse. Of course it can also be sown directly in the garden for summer growing. This is my favorite melon, and it grows prolifically without any black plastic. It is also one of the earliest melons. And best of all, it turns from dark green to orange overnight when it is ripe, so you never have to guess.

PURPLE TOP GLOBE TURNIPS

Not many root vegetables are reliable self-seeders, but this turnip breaks the mold—if every vegetable self-seeded as reliably as this turnip, none of us would ever have to plant a garden again. This heirloom turnip has wonderful taste, is a hardy plant, and is great for using in roast vegetable dishes and soups. There's a beautiful purple ring around a white globe with white flesh inside.

MOUNTAIN ROSE POTATOES

I've fallen in love with this potato. It is extraordinarily early—so early I can grow two harvests a year, three when I use the greenhouse, believe it or not. In 2013, we harvested our first Mountain Rose potatoes from the geothermal greenhouse on Mother's Day for eating—a staggering accomplishment that goes a long way for any house trying to be more self-sufficient. This potato is so cold-hardy and vigorous that it self-seeds simply by accidentally leaving a potato in the ground—or in the straw beds, where I grow my potatoes. Unfortunately, Mountain Rose potatoes can be hard to find. I try to offer a group purchase each spring on SeedRenaissance.com if they are available.

LINDON BIG MAMA TOMATOES

Like the Indian Woman yellow beans I've already mentioned, these tomatoes always seem to replace at least as many plants as the original generation and often add a few more. Perhaps most remarkable of all, these plants start to produce tomatoes when they are four inches tall—but only if they are self-seeded plants. And the plants just keep growing all summer, getting taller and taller, producing tomatoes all the while. Theses tomatoes come up pretty late compared to all the other self-seeders in this chapter, so you have to make sure you don't till or disturb the soil where these grew the year before if you want them to seed for you again—including the nearest pathways.

DWARF SIBERIAN BLUE KALE

I don't ever have to plant kale anymore because my dwarf Siberian blue takes care of itself. If you ask me, any vegetable that takes care of itself tastes twice as nice! This is a beautiful plant with perfect flavor. It is popular for green smoothies, and it is good as a salad ingredient or sautéed by itself as a side dish.

AMERICA SPINACH

This is not only the most cold-hardy spinach I have been able to find, but it is also an extremely reliable self-seeder. At the end of the garden season, let the plants flower and drop their seed, and in a few weeks you will have a whole new crop of spinach—a great blessing. For winter eating, just cover it with a cold frame. My self-seeded autumn America spinach is fully grown and ready to eat by the end of September.

The author's squash harvest.

CHAPTER 15
THE MAGIC FOUR

In my first book, I taught you how to hand-pollinate squashes for backyard seed-saving, which is an essential skill for serious gardeners. But there is an easier way, especially if you are just looking to feed your family and save money on seed. That is to use "the magic four."

Squashes come in four different species, and these four species do not cross with each other. This means that you can plant one kind of each species and harvest the seed without hand-pollinating. They can grow next to each other without cross-pollinating, year after year. No need to worry that the squashes will have crossed with other varieties, which turns the squashes feral in one generation—if Mother Nature has been allowed to mix pollen with a species in your garden, you have no idea what the squashes will look like if you grow out the seed.

All squashes are annuals, and also outbreeding, which means that one squash plant needs to receive pollen from another squash plant instead of a blossom on the same plant for ideal pollination. To avoid genetic depression and maintain vigor, squashes for seed-saving should receive pollen from two or three plants.

Below are descriptions of the four squash species. I am indebted to the book *Seed to Seed* by Suzanne Ashworth, from which I compiled this summary of species lists. Her book has a much larger and more detailed list, and it names all the varieties by individual names, which is beyond the scope of this book.

After each species summary below, I will recommend one variety to be your "magic" squash in that species, meaning you can save seed from it without hand-pollinating. I give my reasons for my choice, but I encourage you to do your own garden trials of different varieties. If you come up with a favorite "magic" squash that is different than mine, email me at calebwarnock@yahoo.com and share your picks and why you chose them. I may share some reader picks on my blog at CalebWarnock.blogspot.com.

1. *Mixta* Squash

Crosses with most varieties of cushaw squashes, all varieties of wild seroria squashes, and silver seed gourds as well as big white crookneck squashes, Cochiti Pueblo squashes, and others. Does not cross with golden cushaw, orange cushaw, or orange-striped cushaw.

CALEB'S RECOMMENDED *MIXTA*: Dishpan cushaw, a medium-sized white-flesh pumpkin with a white or pale-green skin and a good flavor. Stores until January. (Garden trials of cushaw squashes are desperately needed.) This is available at SeedRenaissance.com.

2. *Moschata* Squash

Crosses with all varieties of butternut squashes and cheese squashes, and golden cushaw, orange cushaw, orange-striped cushaw, sweet potato squashes, citrouille d'Eysines, field pumpkins, Futtsu squashes, Kikuza squashes, Landreth squashes, Long Island cheese squashes, Tennessee squashes, Napoli squashes, rampicante (also called *tromboncino*), and others.

CALEB'S RECOMMENDED *MOSCHATA*: Rampicante. This is a wonderful Italian heirloom that is very rare in the United States. Everyone should grow this! It is sweeter than all other zucchinis. The seeds are all contained in a bulb at the end of the squash. It is trumpet-shaped and beautiful. And best of all, if left on the vine, it will slowly begin to change color, flavor, and texture, turning from a summer squash to a winter butternut-type squash that will store until the end of February in a cold room or garage. Available at SeedRenaissance.com.

3. *Pepo* Squash

Crosses with all varieties of summer squashes, acorn squashes, cocozelle squashes, crookneck squashes, scallop squashes, zucchini squashes, vegetable marrow squashes, most gourds, as well as Connecticut field pumpkin, delicata, early prolific straightneck, Fordhook, scallopini squashes, Jack-O'-Lantern, Howden squashes, Japanese pie, Lakota, naked-seeded, New England pie, patisson, potimarron, Rocky Mountain pie, rondo de Nice, straightneck, small sugar squashes, Thelma Sanders, spaghetti squashes (also called vegetable spaghetti), winter pie, Xochitlan Pueblo, and others.

Cushaw pumpkin

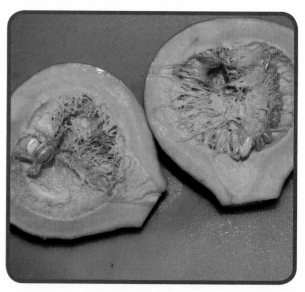

Cut view of potimarron winter squash

CALEB'S RECOMMENDED *PEPO*: Potimarron. I love this squash! It's a teardrop-shaped, dense, intensely red winter squash with fantastic storage. These are on the small side, but they are almost solid with flesh inside—worth growing just for the flavor, but also because these squashes are prolific. Lots of squashes! This remarkable squash—which has been grown for hundreds of years in France—also has some cold-soil tolerance. You can plant it from seed in a cloche or cold frame up to forty-five days before your last frost, so you get a big jump on the squash season.

Now, after reading the variety summary for pepo you might be wondering how anyone could ever choose—after all, choosing one means forgoing summer squashes, Halloween pumpkins like Connecticut field, and even spaghetti squashes. Well, truth be told, it is a hard choice, and maybe your choice will be different than potimarron, which is my recommendation. Here is my logic. Rampicante (my pick for the *moschata* species) is a great summer squash zucchini, so that covers zucchini. If you want summer yellow squashes, or other summer zucchini, they are so easy to come by, you can get them for free from neighbors, friends, family, or your local Freecycle.org group. You could even buy them, because in season they are very inexpensive. You can also buy Halloween pumpkins for carving, or get them from Freecycle members. Same with spaghetti squashes. They are all available without too much work or expense. But potimarron is much harder to come by, it is a mainstay winter squash, it produces huge amounts of squashes, and it's one of the two most delicious winter squashes I've ever tasted (Mormon pumpkin being the other). And it stores into February or March with the right conditions. Potimarron goes a long way toward self-sufficiency and flavor, so it's my pick for pepo. Available at SeedRenaissance.com

Mature rampicante zucchini

4. *Maxima* Squash

Crosses with all banana squash varieties, buttercup squash varieties, Hubbard squash varieties, Turban squash varieties, and marrow squash varieties, as well as Amish pie, Australian pumpkin, Mormon pumpkin, and others.

CALEB'S RECOMMENDED *MAXIMA*: Mormon pumpkin. I am the only person in the world to offer this commercially (SeedRenaissance.com). This squash was saved from extinction only by a hair. Originally grown by the Mormon pioneers, this invaluable squash came to me through one family; they saved the seeds and gave them to a neighbor, who gave them to me. This squash exceeded all my expectations. The outside is a rare dusty green with hints of gray (the unusual color is almost identical to the 1719 wood paneling from a Paris townhouse built by the architect to Louis XIV, now on display at the Getty Center in Los Angeles). The pumpkin shell also shows occasional streaks of orange. The inside is solid orange, and the flesh is sweet, dense, and thick. I got four and a half quarts of puree from a single one of these squashes, the size of my head! The flavor is great—we love it in soup, pumpkin bars, pumpkin waffles, and pumpkin cookies. It stores well. I'm very proud to offer this squash to the public for the first time in memory! I'm grateful to the family that saved it from extinction and gave it to me.

CHAPTER 16
GARDEN TRIALS:
FROM BEGINNERS TO G.R.I.N.

On December 17, 2012, I planted the following in my geothermal greenhouse:

- Twenty-two varieties of rare heirloom lettuce
- Eighteen varieties of mostly rare heirloom peas
- Two rare strawberries from seed
- Two varieties of cucumber
- A half-dozen types of untypical salad greens

Just coming up with the seed for the trials had taken a lot of time and money, and now the real work began: studying the seeds' growth to judge cold-soil tolerance. From the day they were planted until the day they were finished and died (it's now seven months later, and some of them are still going), I kept a careful log of their progress—the first to sprout, height measurements at intervals, lots of photo and video documentation, which varieties were edible first, which resisted heat best, which struggled in the cold soil the worst (or never germinated at all), colors of flowers, and notes on flavors, colors, and form. It was months of work.

Why bother?

For starters, I love to do it. I love working with plants. It makes me happy. I've always worked with plants, since I was a boy, and I hope to continue for many decades to come, God willing (please). I started doing this work out of frustration, because my garden season is exceptionally short. Knowing my day counts and soil temperature tolerances was the only thing between me and failure after I moved to my current home just over a decade ago. I had been used to gardening in a longer season with better established soil.

Mostly, however, I do this because the work is important. Thousands of people have now benefited from my work. Many of them have completely changed the way they garden after examining my methods and successes, which they have accessed in my classes, in my books, on my blog, and through the seed varieties that "win" my garden trials and are then offered for sale at SeedRenaissance.com. I am fortunate to now regularly get mail, email, and online messages thanking me for my work, often with pictures and descriptions of how these people have been able to put my hard-won information to work in their own life—whether it be my hundreds of hours of research about natural yeast or my work to save some of the rarest seeds in the world or my work to revive the lost art of winter gardening.

Cold soil tolerance trial for beans.

I run a lot of these kinds of tests, and I spend thousands of dollars doing it. This kind of work, whether on a large scale or small, used to be popular. I love to go back a century and read the old gardening periodicals, where everyday gardeners like me would write in and report their trials and successes and failures so that gardeners everywhere could benefit. I love the community spirit in these missives from the past, the respect for craft, the dedication to the greater good, the passion for good food, and the love and curiosity for the natural world. I would have fit right in with those people a century ago. We would have been friends. I look forward to looking up some of these people when I move on to the next realm. I hope that I'm allowed to check out the video of their lives from the Next Realm Library. I can think of thousands of people whose lives I would like to study in the Next Realm, where I won't need to worry about weeding—right?!

For an example of these old articles, here are a couple of snippets from the December 1926 *Gardeners' Chronicle of America*:

"The Vegetable Garden" by John Carman

"Early January is not too early to sow onion seeds, where specimens are required for exhibition purposes. A long growing season is essential in producing onions which can win with keen competition. Sowing early and growing comparatively cool with careful watering are steps in the right direction."[1]

"Your Work under Glass" by William S. Ellis

"Lilacs for forcing may be given temperatures of 45 degrees about the first of the year. It is not advisable to attempt to force lilacs that were used for this purpose last year. It is safer to purchase stock that were grown expressly for forcing or to utilize plants that have not been permitted to flower for two years. When the buds begin to swell, increase the heat, moisture, and water proportionately."[2]

Returning to the modern day (do we have to?), let me pose some questions:

- What vegetable varieties do not thrive in alkaline soil, and which aren't bothered by alkalinity?

- Which root vegetables thrive in cold soil?

- Which lettuces resist the heat of summer best?

- Which grow best under the shade of a tree in summer?

- Which squash tastes better in winter storage?

- Which melon stays sugary longest in storage?

- Which carrot grows fastest?

- Which heirloom brassica varieties are the most resistant to aphids?

- Which tomato freezes best?

- Which bean produces the best flavor in alkaline soil? Or the biggest bean? What bean has the highest protein content, making it best for winter chicken feed (after being soaked)?

- What is the best short-season edamame?

- Is there a reliable self-seeding watermelon?

- Which strawberry produces earliest? Longest? Has the best flavor?

- What vegetables produce best at high elevations?

I could fill a book with these kinds of questions, and you could likely add some of your own that I haven't thought of. I'm working on the answers to some of these, but more garden questions need answering than I will ever live long enough to tackle. The single greatest source of questions comes from microclimates, which have been almost totally ignored in our rush to label zones and produce only "national" vegetable varieties. The more detailed information we have, the better produce we can grow. Ideally, we would have information about vegetables according to soil type, shade, elevation, and water requirements. For example, ideally we would know what is the shortest day count tomato at what elevation increment. There are so many gaps in our information about day counts alone—and lack of knowledge and experience with day counts is probably the single biggest reason beginning gardeners give up or fail. Yet almost no gardener I have ever met can even give the correct definition of day count (remember: the number of days from when the vegetable opens its true leaves to the day it first produces fruit).

The answer to all these questions is garden trials. Any gardener can run a trial, and every gardener should run at least one a year, no matter how small. Learning the varieties that work best in your garden is information that can help everyone around you. Here's how to get started:

1. Small trials are valuable. Every trial is useful and moves garden knowledge forward. Here are some suggestions that just scratch the surface of what is possible:

- Plant three kinds of tomatoes on the same day and observe which produces the first tomato.

Winter vegetable trials in the author's unheated geo-thermal greenhouse.

Peas on January 15 in the author's unheated geothermal greenhouse.

• With your friends and family, do a taste test of three or more kinds of tomatoes, carrots, lettuce, potatoes, green beans—any vegetable.

• Plant three kinds of cucumbers and observe which produces first. Put all three in the fridge and see which stays crisp longest. Observe which kind produces the largest number of cucumbers per plant. Or which plant produces cukes latest into the fall. Or which cucumber make the best refrigerator pickles. Or all of these.

• Have a taste test of apple varieties from your trees and the trees of several neighbors. (Be sure everyone knows the variety of their apples, or the results won't help anyone.)

• Plant three kinds of lettuce under the deep shade of a tree in June and see which thrives best.

• Plant three types of pole or bush beans and see which produces first. Or most prolifically. Or has the best flavor when raw or cooked.

2. Choose a vegetable you are interested in. If you love tomatoes, test different varieties. If you love melons, work with those. Do whatever garden trial will get you excited.

3. Document your results, whether on a blog or on Facebook or in a garden journal.

• Write down dates. When you planted, when you harvested, when your plants produced flowers.

• Keep track of day counts. This is perhaps the most valuable information of all. To keep an accurate day count, you will need to write down the date you planted the seed, the date it produced true leaves (the second set of leaves), and the date it produced its first ripe fruit or first fruit large enough to harvest.

• Take photos. They don't have to be professional or stylish or perfect. Any clear photo will do.

Make sure you know what date you took the photo.

4. Use only heirloom (open-pollinated) varieties. Hybrids are owned by corporations and patent-holders. You will always have to pay for that seed, which is not the goal of self-sufficiency. And since some company is making money off those patents and trademarks, let them do their own tests and trials. Heirloom varieties are largely ignored and dying out, yet they stand to help the largest number of people because heirloom seed can legally be saved, bartered, or gifted. No money required. If you are not sure whether a variety is heirloom or not, don't use it. Every seed I sell at SeedRenaissance.com is guaranteed heirloom and pure.

5. Share your results, even if they are incomplete or inconclusive. Sharing on a blog is a great solution. Or share with a local gardening group, whether in person, on a Facebook page, or on another website. Many areas of the country have Facebook gardening groups where people share photos and information online about their garden successes and problems, and they help each other by answering questions or recommending varieties. If you can't find such a group in your area, start one. You can also find garden clubs, some of them new and some in existence for decades, that are always looking for new, excited members. Whatever you do, don't keep your garden trial results to yourself. You can even email them to me and I'll share them on my blog. Calebwarnock@yahoo.com.

6. After you've had some experience with small trials, you might decide you are up to a larger trail, maybe ten varieties at a time (or whatever number you think you can sustain) or several small trials simultaneously. Wonderful! If you are at this level and excited by this challenge, you should join Seed Savers Exchange, which is a group of volunteers around the world working to save the last varieties of heirloom seeds before they vanish. In many cases, only one or two people in the world are keeping a variety alive. Joining SSE will give you access to tens of thousands of seed varieties you can get nowhere else and will link you to a network of like-minded gardeners. When you get the annual yearbook, you will be able to see at a glance who around the world is working with what varieties—who is devoting all their time to heirloom sweet potatoes, for example, or rutabaga or oil seed pumpkins (oil seed pumpkins are an area where attention is desperately needed). You will also be able to see messages from aging keepers of seed who say frankly, "This is the last year I will be able to list this seed," because of poor health or of advancing age or they have lost their home to bankruptcy—and if that seed is one you are interested in, you can jump in and help keep it from extinction. You can trial varieties and report your results in the annual yearbook, where the results will be documented and preserved for generations. The number of people doing this work is small, but the need is enormous.

7. For advanced work, you could take on landrace or other banked varieties from the US Germplasm Resources Information Network (GRIN), which is basically the federal seed bank program. GRIN is an arm of the National Genetic Resources Program, which was created by Congress in 1990 to "acquire, characterize, preserve, document, and distribute to scientists, germplasm of all lifeforms important for food and agricultural production."[3] GRIN's online catalog has descriptions of thousands and thousands of seeds, most of which have not been studied or grown in garden environments. GRIN does grow out the seed in small amounts periodically to keep it viable. These seeds are not seeds from catalogs.

Trialing tomato varieties to see which ripen best in winter storage.

Rather, most of them are considered landrace seeds, meaning they were collected from the wild, most often from other countries. Landrace seeds are the genetic nursery for creating new vegetable varieties or re-creating traits—such as extreme winter tolerance—that vegetables once had but have since been lost to extinction. The possibilities with landrace seed and raw germplasm (untested, unstable seed) are endless, but they take work. Creating a new, stable vegetable variety—or breeding for certain traits—can be rewarding and frustrating. The most important thing for you to know is that almost no one is doing this work. Corporations and scientists have access to the germplasm bank, and they use that access to create hybrid, patented, and trademarked varieties—and you could to, if that was your heart's desire. But for thousands of years, people created and bred vegetables to benefit mankind, leaving them open-pollinated but stable so the seed could be saved by families anywhere as long as they knew how. I am one of only a handful of people in the United States—perhaps less than a handful—who are working without pay to create new open-pollinated vegetable varieties. My focus is on winter vegetables, because so many of the most important varieties have already gone extinct. Your focus would be wherever your passion is.

If you have some experience and confidence with the first six suggestions I have listed here and you have a desire to work with germplasm, you are needed. You should start by reading the most important modern book on this subject, *Breed Your Own Vegetable Varieties* by Carol Deppe, who is a national treasure, and that is no exaggeration. Her book will teach you the basics of how to get involved in the federal germplasm program. A small introduction from me here will be less helpful than the full introduction in her book, so I won't go into further details. But I will say this. I work with the federal germplasm program, and there is a lot of important work to do. No one will assign you any task—that is not how the program works. The work you want to tackle is up to you, and the more you show germplasm program managers the results of your work, the more they will give you access to the germplasm, which is limited and expensive to maintain but given to qualified corporations and backyard gardeners alike without charge.

Notes

1. Carman, "The Vegetable Garden."

2. Ellis, "Your Work Under Glass."

3. Germplasm Resources Information Network, "Welcome!"

CHAPTER 17
FIVE MYSTERIES
OF THE GARDEN

1. Is Noir des Carmes cantaloupe self-pollinating?

It certainly appears to be after my years of study. Noir des Carmes—which is my favorite cantaloupe on earth—is what scientists call "andromonoecious," which means that it has two kinds of flowers on the same plant: some that are only male and some that are "perfect," also known as hermaphrodite—both male and female reproductive organs in the same flower. Why andromonoecious plants have some flowers that are only male is a mystery. What is the biological purpose? Scientists haven't figured out the answer yet. But for a cantaloupe to be self-pollinating is unheard of, which is why I still don't announce it to the world—I'd be laughed at. (Okay, I guess I'm kind of announcing it to the world right now—but I'm qualifying it with "it appears to be.")

In the scientific world, the "perfect" flowers on cantaloupes are considered to be unable to self-pollinate, and insects are necessary. In fact, most of the time cantaloupe flowers are able to be pollinated only for a few hours, and in hot weather, only for a few minutes. But three pieces of fairly strong evidence suggest to me that Noir des Carmes seems to be self-pollinating.

First, I've had Noir des Carmes pollinate and form fruit in my geothermal greenhouse in winter when there are no bees or other insects around that I've been able to discern, and I did not hand-pollinate. (I have also hand-pollinated Noir des Carmes).

Second, the Noir des Carmes in my garden has never crossed with any other cantaloupes, whether

Noir des Carmes cantaloupe turns orange overnight when the cantaloupe is ripe.

growing in my garden or growing in a neighbor's—and that is unheard of.

Third, Noir des Carmes was grown in winter hotbeds covered in glass for hundreds of years. I have scoured the old literature, and there is not a single mention of any hand-pollination or somehow adding pollinating insects in winter. In fact, to my knowledge hand-pollination was not known to the world four hundred years ago.

It's a mystery to me. One day I'd like to be able to prove my theory. If you have any thoughts or useful information, email me at calebwarnock@yahoo.com.

2. What makes a cold-season variety possible?

Why does red iceberg lettuce sprout so well in a January hotbed while Ice Queen lettuce does not? Why does Vernal Red orach simply love cold weather? Why will a Broad Windsor fava produce flowers outside in below-freezing temperatures

Winter spinach growing in the author's garden.

while most beans won't even sprout? The mechanics of what makes one vegetable variety a cold-season winner and another crave warm soil are a mystery. What we do know for sure is that there were a lot more cold-season vegetables available several hundred years ago. Unfortunately most are extinct today because winter gardening became all but extinct itself after the invention of the modern grocery store.

3. Why does compost in the West slowly turn to clay?

Gardeners with years of composting experience, including me, who also live in the western United States in areas with clay soil have noticed a fascinating phenomena—loamy compost eventually turns into clay soil just like the native soil. How is this happening? I suspect the answer lies with the type of enzymes dominant in the natural setting. After all, Mother Nature has been producing evaporation-resistant clay soils in water-starved areas long before man appeared. She knows what she's doing. But how she's doing it remains a mystery. Having the loamy compost you've patiently worked for slowly turn to clay can be frustrating. Luckily, there is a fairly easy solution—add sand to the compost. Vermiculite and perlite help too.

4. What are we going to do about the bees?

My peach tree produced no peaches this year, not a single one. It's alarming. There were no bees. I never saw or heard a bee on this tree the entire time it was flowering, which is strange for our yard. There are a lot of theories about why bee populations are crashing. I have my own. Beekeeping has become so unnatural—feeding bees sugar water, providing man-made hive materials, greedily taking too much of the honey they need to survive the winter, spraying chemicals everywhere in the natural environment, killing off the weeds that produce early flowers for spring food (dandelions) and late flowers for autumn food (dandelions again, wild mustards). Few "natural" hives are left—when was the last time you saw an actual bee colony living in a hollow in a tree, even deep in the mountains? Bees are so important to pollination, so what are we going to do without the bees? Is there anything sadder than a beautiful peach tree void of fruit? The world is going to be a hungry place if this decline in bee population continues much longer.

5. What makes a short-season vegetable variety possible?

If all vegetables were short-season varieties, we could dramatically increase yields with succession plantings and longer harvest times. If you have a 120-day tomato and a 60-day tomato, the 60-day tomato is going to produce fruit for 60 days longer than the first variety! Which begs the question, what makes one tomato produce fruit in 60 days and another one take twice as long? I understand that short-season varieties are the result of centuries of breeding work done by interested gardeners, but what is it that makes the genetics of one plant work so much faster than the genetics of another variety? It is a mystery.

Bees feasting on purple coneflowers in the author's garden.

When bones are used as fertilizer in the garden, nothing is wasted.

CHAPTER 18
WANT TO LIVE GREEN?
KILL A ROOSTER

Earlier this week, I killed a snake. Reluctantly. I'm not in the habit of killing snakes. Garden snakes, also called garter snakes, are a wonderful organic pest control, and a lot of fun too. They feed primarily on slugs, and they are the perfect snake because they don't have teeth and don't bite. Garter snakes eat squash bugs, tomato worms, and baby mice, so they are an organic gardener's dream.

When winter arrives, our *Henries*, as we call the garter snakes who have adopted our yard, move themselves into the geothermal greenhouse through a hole in the wall. The Henries are three years old now and had spring babies. Earlier this week at the time of this writing, I found not one, not three, but six Henries slithering around the vegetables I was trying to weed. Six is a lot of snakes in a 108-square-foot greenhouse. And the Henries have gotten big—the original three are each about three feet long.

I didn't mind much, but my wife thought the math of six snakes in one small greenhouse didn't add up satisfactorily. After a bout of existential angst, I picked up a Henry and broke its neck.

I did it because, like its life, our serpent friend's death benefits my garden. I buried Henry's body in the compost pit. Over the next twelve months, the body will devolve into next year's black gold.

Which brings me to killing roosters.

We eat our chickens. Which means that someone in our family (me) has to take the ax out to the pasture and—how shall I say this?—remove the chicken's head. Because this topic makes some would-be greenies queasy, I like to call the process the "Sunday dinner solution."

Why the queasiness? Harvesting a chicken is not bad for the environment. Paying someone else to harvest your chicken—in other words, buying it at the grocery store—is. Herein lies a tension point about what it really means to live green.

In the back pages of the December 1930 issue of *Gardeners' Chronicle of America*, now long defunct, is a four-inch by three-inch ad for "Bon Arbor Half Inch Cracked-Bone" touting the fertilizer qualities of digging bone into your backyard garden: "Is used extensively for Fall planting of Roses, Graperies, Trees and Shrubbery to insure healthy growth

The author's grandson, Xander, cuddling a chick hatched by one of the author's hens. As expected, half of all chicks are male.

The author's granddaughter, Ada, makes a habit of feasting on fresh tomatoes any time she is allowed into the garden to pick them.

through slow feeding," reads the ad. "The roots will cling to this cracked bone, which gradually feeds them and will be found to remain in the ground several years. We have an unlimited stock of the nicest grade of cracked bone, for immediate shipment. Price: $12 per 200-pound barrel."[1]

When this magazine issue was new, organic gardening was just beginning to lose its place as the assumption. Industrial-scale hybrid seed and plants were recent inventions. Companies were beginning to spend big money to convince backyard gardeners that chemicals were the wisdom of the future. Alongside the ads for things like sheep manure, bonemeal, "Blue Ribbon Guano," and "Ground Tobacco Stems: Cleaner and better than manure," other things began to appear, like Scaline—"a dormant spray to kill Scale, Aphis eggs, etc."—and "Wilson's Scale-O . . . so necessary to the successful growth of fruit and other trees."

The chemical era had dawned.

The modern green vogue has not yet revived the kind of gardening where half-inch cracked bone is lauded. But it should be. At our house, we have ten to thirty chickens free-ranging our pasture at any given time. Keeping chickens brings the cycle of life and death into full view: In the depth of winter, wild creatures see our chickens as their hunger-gap salvation. Even the most careful owner of free-range chickens finds a carcass from time to time. And if you keep a rooster (we have four right now) then you know that roosters love reproducing, which means chicks. But half of all chicks grow up to be roosters.

Nationwide interest in the homestead movement is growing. But little or nothing is being said about the art of culling—the preferred euphemism for killing unwanted roosters. We must not shy away. Our sin of omission is not helping our cause.

Roosters are territorial and loud, they eat a lot,

and they lay no eggs. Whether you look at roosters through the lens of money or space or noise, keeping a bunch of roosters doesn't compute. So you can see where this is going. There are going to be some carcasses.

Blood, when composted, becomes a high-nitrogen fertilizer. So blood and guts go into the compost pit. Chicken feathers are almost pure nitrogen, so in goes the skin and feathers. (We never pluck our chickens; we're not that into eating the skin.) Bone is high in phosphorus, so the bones go into the compost pit.

In other words, not a feather nor a blood cell is wasted when we harvest a chicken for the dinner table or cull a rooster. And there is no stink, because the carcass is buried in the compost pit.

Now compare that to what happens when you bring your chicken home from the grocery store. The head is still removed from the chicken, but you pay someone else to do that. The chicken is put on a Styrofoam tray and covered in plastic. The bagger puts the entire package into another plastic film bag, to protect against leaking blood. This then goes into a plastic grocery sack. Whatever happens to the blood, guts, feathers, and bones is a mystery—or at least the meat industry would like you to think it is. In reality, some is made into pet food and some is ground up and used for farm animal feed—if anything makes you queasy, that should be it. Four different pieces of plastic have been used, and you and I both know that none of them is going into your recycle bin at home, and they shouldn't, because they have blood on them.

One last green benefit of harvesting your chicken dinner at home: you know what your dinner ate, which means you know what you are eating. In May 2012, the Washington Post reported that Maryland was set to become the first state in the nation to ban arsenic-based drugs from chicken feed.[2] In a 2006 report titled *Playing Chicken: Arsenic in Your Meat*, David Wallinga and the Institute for Agriculture and Trade Policy found that at least 70 percent of all US chickens raised for meat are fed arsenic.[3] Industrial farms use arsenic compounds to fatten turkeys, chickens, and pigs and to improve pigmentation.

But when you can handle your own meat—from hatching, through life, and then through death—you know what is in your chicken. No antibiotics, no arsenic, no hormones, no chemicals, no mechanically processed feed. (I feed my chickens whole wheat; if you feed your chickens store-bought chicken feed, I would recommend you do not compost your chickens.)

Notes

1. "Bon Arbor Half Inch Cracked-Bone," *Gardener's Chronicle of America*.

2. Fears, "Maryland Set to Ban Arsenic-Containing Drug in Chicken Feed."

3. Wallinga, *Playing Chicken*, 5.

A view of the author's backyard.

CHAPTER 19
DEAR CALEB:
REAL QUESTIONS FROM READERS

QUESTION: Caleb, we want to be more self-sufficient when it comes to eating. How much space do we need for a garden?

ANSWER: No offense, but you are asking the wrong question. The real question is how much space do you have time to manage right now. How much space will you really, truly use? I have an elderly neighbor who got all excited about gardening one day and paid a couple thousand dollars to have someone come over and build her a huge raised bed—probably forty feet long and ten feet wide—and then paid someone to bring in garden soil to fill it. She used it once, and it has grown weeds ever since. The kids these days call that an "epic fail." Start small and manageable. Remember, change you cannot sustain is the same as failure, only it usually costs more! You can double your effort later. If you are really itching to make a "big" change, then satiate yourself with a five-year plan. Maybe this year you will grow a self-sufficient number of carrots and lettuce. Next year, onions, potatoes, carrots, and lettuce.

QUESTION: Are you aware of any place where people can get free mulch?

ANSWER: Electrical and utility companies send trucks around to trim trees that are encroaching on power lines, and they will usually drop off a load at no charge at the request of a resident if they are cutting and grinding trees in the area.

QUESTION: Caleb, have you had any problem with chickens eating their eggs? Why do they do this and what can we do to prevent it?

ANSWER: Chickens sometimes start eating eggs because they are bored, and usually when they are locked in a coop and are not free-range. Feed them more, and gather the eggs two times a day if possible to get them out of the habit. Put several wooden eggs in the nest boxes—this encourages the chickens to lay more eggs, but it also discourages eating eggs because if you gather the eggs two times a day for a couple of weeks, the egg-eating chicken will quickly find she is not having much success with the wooden eggs and she should get over it. If the chicken is not bored, eating eggs is usually a sign of calcium deficiency or protein deficiency or both. Make sure you are feeding the chickens their eggshells back, and give them oyster shells if necessary (or ask your neighbors to save their eggshells for you). Give the chickens kitchen vegetable scraps every day to vary their diet.

QUESTION: What would you advise for those of us who do not have access to the secret pioneer harvesting spot for asparagus? Our uncle got us turned onto the idea of planting our own, but it turns out that the plants from the source he recommended, from [redacted company name], are actually hybrid. Would you have any thoughts on that?

ANSWER: I love this question. I have two answers. The first is that, as I mentioned in my first Forgotten Skills book, I grew up eating from the huge original pioneer asparagus stands in my hometown, which flourish to this day. The reason they flourish is that they are open-pollinated and not hybrid. If the pioneers had chosen to plant hybrid asparagus (which wasn't even an option for them, as it did not exist) those plants would be long gone. Instead, more than a century later, they are still yielding spectacularly—and they will be producing a century from now.

Why? Because modern hybrid plants last about a decade. Heirloom open-pollinated plants last forever. (The asparagus have a summer water source in Utah's desert climate—they are planted on the ditch banks in my hometown). They last forever because they slowly reseed themselves if you let them (in wet climates, they seed prolifically). The original pioneer plants in my hometown are long gone—we are now eating from self-planted child plants generations

down the line. What a wonderful gift from the pioneers! Free food for an entire town for more than a century! And it tastes so much better than any asparagus you ever get in a store, by far.

My second answer to your question is that there really is no such thing as a hybrid asparagus.

I say this reluctantly, so let me explain. Asparagus is a perennial plant, and there is no true hybrid perennial in the modern sense of the word. Hybrid, in the sense that you and I use the word, means self-suiciding, patented, and corporate owned. Hybrid asparagus is patented and corporate owned, but it is NOT self-suiciding because it is perennial, and that is the crucial part. I have hybrid Jersey asparagus growing in my own garden, where I grow NO hybrid plants—readers of my books know I don't believe in hybrid vegetables. For the record, I also have heirloom Martha Washington asparagus in my garden, for reasons I will explain in a moment. Hybrid asparagus does not propagate through seeds, like heirloom asparagus. Hybrid asparagus propagates vegetatively by cutting, as does heirloom asparagus. So if you can find someone with an established patch of any kind of asparagus, and if they don't mind, you can go in carefully with a razor blade knife and take free cuttings and plant them in your own garden—and then you can grow those out and share them, and those people can share them, and we can feed the whole community without ever having to purchase asparagus, even if they are patented hybrids. The law says we can give away patented hybrid cuttings from plants on our own property; we just can't sell them.

Because I try to give full information, let me say that there is a small risk when transplanting asparagus—you could import a garden virus or disease into your garden from the host garden. All asparagus plants that you buy in stores—whether heirloom or hybrid—are not grown from seed or cuttings. They are actually grown from tissue samples cultured in test tubes in sterile laboratories because the seller could be legally liable if the plant you buy is infected with a virus or disease and it spreads in your garden and then your community. (This is also how seed potatoes are grown and why they cost so much!) By law, companies are not allowed to sell real roots (crowns) for this reason.

I'm not really afraid of transplanting diseases by taking (or giving) free cuttings. My thought is that if you get the cuttings from someone fairly local to you, you have very little chance of transplanting anything into your garden that you don't already have. So long as the cuttings you take are local and from obviously healthy plants, I think cuttings are the way to go.

One last caution. Remember, if you want your asparagus patch to feed people for centuries, that can only be accomplished with open-pollinated varieties like Mary Washington and Martha Washington. Hybrid plants, even from cuttings, will die and have to be replaced within your lifetime, probably several times. Of greater concern to me (and the reason I have heirloom asparagus in my own garden along with the all-male hybrids) is that preserving a thriving genetic community of asparagus is very important. Because they are tissue cultures, all commercially sold asparagus plants—whether heirloom or hybrid—are clones. Cloning is a perfect genetic bottleneck. With asparagus, cloning is not a huge issue outside of Utah because heirloom asparagus has naturalized on both coasts, providing a vibrant genetically stable source for future generations. But in Utah, the only genetically stable open-pollinated asparagus is in the closely guarded pioneer patches. (Where you might get shot by a local for thievery if you attempted to take cuttings without permission. And getting permission is highly unlikely. I'm

a native and I haven't dared to take cuttings!) In Utah and everywhere in the arid West, we desperately need more genetically vibrant open-pollinated source stock for asparagus, which you would be helping to provide if you planted heirloom plants in your garden because heirloom varieties produce half male and half female plants (roughly), and those plants produce true seed. This stock exists in abundance throughout the rest of the United States, but it is not easily accessible to us here (except as imported wildcrafted seed) because of distance and because we might very well be importing disease (not to mention weed seeds) if we had someone send us crown cuttings (or even seed).

Indulge me in a related matter for a moment. It is important to note that very few potatoes produce true seed anymore, and potatoes all across the United States are now at a severe genetic bottleneck, which is causing rampant loss to disease and makes it difficult (but not impossible) for organic growers like me to maintain excellent seed stock. Potatoes grown with commercial fertilizer do not work well as seed stock in organic gardens because they are so genetically weak—they depend almost entirely on petroleum-derived processed fertilizer because they no longer work well with the natural soil mycelium, which organic growers depend on for soil fertility. This is a serious problem in the United States that is getting almost no attention. Breeding strong potatoes for the organic garden from true seed is a critical need that no one in the United States is working on to my knowledge. (I have just started working on it. I got true potato seed from a friend in England. I also have rare heirloom potato varieties now growing in my garden that produce true seed.)

Back to asparagus. You can find Youtube videos demonstrating how to take asparagus cuttings. However, none of those videos demonstrate the way

I would do it. I disagree with removing and cutting up the entire plant. There is no reason to remove the entire plant because now you have a bunch of cuttings that will need to grow without being harvested for three years—asparagus transplants will die if harvested before the third year because the root must be fed enough by the plant to allow the root to mature for perennial overwintering. It would be better if the cuttings were taken carefully from the source plant without disturbing the rest of the root system—then the owner of the source plant still gets their regular harvest from the roots left behind. Also, in some videos they choose to take only male plants, which means they have basically created hybrid transplants, whether the source plant was hybrid or not. Taking some males and some females would give you the genetically heirloom, seed-producing asparagus I mention above.

QUESTION: Which crops would you suggest focusing on if you had a small lot? I've planted a lot of raspberries and blackberries, but I like your suggestion [in *Backyard Winter Gardening*] about the Keepsake apples, so I'm looking into those.

ANSWER: Short-season vegetables in raised bed boxes will give you the most eating for the least work and expense. For the full list of my recommended vegetables, visit SeedRenaissance.com, which is my seed website. I only sell seeds I have tested and fallen in love with, and I tell you the reason why I chose each variety.

If you have a small lot, it is even more important to grow short-season vegetables so you maximize the time you spend harvesting as opposed to growing. With little space, a prolonged harvest is key.

QUESTION: Would you ever be willing to sell pre-cut sheets of the greenhouse plastic you buy. I want to build a couple more cold frames like we received in your backyard class last fall, but do not have the means to transport a giant sheet of plastic from wherever it is you buy it.

ANSWER: Due to popular demand, I have started selling the twin-wall polycarbonate sheets for cold frames, with instructions, at SeedRenaissance.com. Twin-wall polycarbonate withstands children (and garden visitors) better than glass, although glass works just as well, as I explain in *Backyard Winter Gardening*.

QUESTION: You are the seed man. How do you store your seeds?

ANSWER: I don't. I plant my seeds. While they are waiting to be planted, I keep them in a handheld plastic file box. The seeds that I grow or purchase for my garden don't last more than a year or two because I plant so many seeds, so long-term storage is not anything I ever worry about—I'm always growing new seed every year. But if you want to store seeds long-term, the best way is to seal them inside three plastic freezer bags, remove as much air as possible, and then freeze them. They will last many years when stored like this, although the germination rate will decline a little each year. Another alternative is to put your seeds in a root cellar or in the bottom of the hole where your outdoor water main is, which should be about four feet deep if you live somewhere with frost. Just make sure they are in something absolutely watertight. Moisture, light, and temperature fluctuations will cause seed to go bad.

CHAPTER 20
LESSONS LEARNED

I thought I would finish off this book with a collection of lessons I've learned the hard way. These are lessons I wish I had known earlier in life. The good news is, I know them now. And after reading this chapter, you will too!

HOW TO PICK A BLACKBERRY

By the end of August, blackberries have been a wonderful treat for weeks at our house. For a long time, before I had my own blackberry bushes, I was only familiar with blackberries purchased from farmers' markets. In other words, they were tart. Turns out, though, that backyard blackberries are not supposed to be tart. In fact, they are a mouthful of sugar if they are picked correctly.

Most people pick their blackberries when they turn black. Wrong! I understand why they are doing this—for a long time, before they are mature, blackberries on the cane are as red as raspberries. When the first berries turn from green to bright red, it's really hard to stop yourself from picking some of the red berries. After all, raspberry season has just ended, and the red blackberries look so delicious. But you

Blackberries are never tart if you know the secret to harvesting them.

put one in your mouth and you pucker. So then you wait until the red blackberries turn black and you think to yourself, "Ah-ha they are ripe!" And you pick them, but they are still mostly tart.

The key is to wait until the blackberries are soft to the touch. When they are finally soft to the touch, they are pure sugar without a trace of tartness. The other wonderful thing about blackberries is that they are enormous. Raspberries are great, but they are small by comparison. When you pick a ripe, sweet blackberry, it's like a quarter cup of juice in your mouth. It's unbelievable.

Now you never have to have a tart blackberry again. And if you don't have a blackberry bush, go get one or five!

I'VE BEEN FOOLED (SECRET HYBRID VEGETABLES)

- Crimson Sweet watermelon
- Speckled Hound winter squash
- Purple Haze carrots

What do these three vegetables have in common? They fooled me.

If you've read my first Forgotten Skills book or been to one of my classes, you know that I don't use hybrid seed in my garden. Why? Because for thousands of years, vegetable seed was free. Then, in the 1920s, someone figured out that if you crossed a vegetable using artificial-pollination methods and kept the parentage secret, you could sell people a new kind of seed, and they and their children and their grandchildren forever more would be forced to buy seed every year.

Hybrid seed was invented to take money away from families who want to be self-sufficient.

"But wait!" you say (and plenty of people have said this to me in my classes). "Hybrid seed is wonderful. It's better!"

"How so?"

"Well," they sputter. "It resists disease better."

"Nope."

"It produces larger crops."

"Nope."

"But, ah, hem, haw—hybrids are better," they say.

"Who told you that?" I ask. "The companies who sell hybrid seed, that's who. And it's not true."

A light bulb begins to go on.

Hybrids were invented to force people to pay for seed. They were invented for money. And if you want to buy hybrid seed, that is fine. Pay for seed for the rest of your life if you want—I don't care. Here is what I do care about. Open-pollinated (heirloom) seed is vanishing. As I discussed in my first book, 94 percent of the varieties sold in garden seed catalogs in the United States in 1903 are now gone forever. Extinct. Because they have been replaced by hybrids. Because hybrids can be patented. Hybrids can be legally controlled to make sure only the creator can sell them. Open-pollinated seed cannot. Open-pollinated seed can be saved by anyone who knows the four methods for saving pure seed (taught in my first book).

Getting rid of the free seed to force people to buy hybrids is greedy and wrong.

Hybrid seeds are self-suiciding. Some vegetables grown from hybrid seed will not produce seed at all (think seedless watermelons). Some will produce seed, but that seed will not resemble the parent—you never know what you will get. There is a well-known garden author in my area who goes around giving lots of classes, and he tells people that you can save seed from hybrid tomatoes to plant in your garden, and those seeds produce tomatoes just fine. And in most cases, he is right—for a single generation. If you save hybrid tomato seeds and plant them, they will be off-color and off-taste in the first generation, but they will produce tomatoes. By the second generation, they are vastly different from the original tomatoes, and by the third generation, they are often small and tasteless and dark colored. So this guy in my area clearly has never tried to save hybrid tomato seed for more than one generation (one generation is one garden-planting season).

Hybrid seed is designed specifically to be unreproducible at home. So you have to buy your garden seed from someone.

Problem is, telling which seeds are hybrid is not always easy. Within the past two years, three seeds have fooled me. In many cases, hybrid seed is simply not labeled.

Take Crimson Sweet watermelon. I bought this seed on a whim in a store one day. It was labeled organic, and I know better than anyone that organic has nothing to do with not being hybrid—organic seed can be hybrid all day long. (Organic just means the seed was grown without chemicals.) But I guess I was off my game on this day because for some reason I thought the seed packet said heirloom. But it didn't. I started these watermelons in my greenhouse, and they were four inches tall before I accidentally discovered, while looking at a seed catalog, that I was growing a hybrid melon. I gave the plants away.

Speckled Hound winter squash has been a real sore spot for me this year. It is growing in my garden right now, and it is beautiful. But no one knows whether it is hybrid or not. The company I originally bought the seed from sold it as open-pollinated (heirloom) seed. Weeks later, I stumbled upon another source that says it is hybrid. I've since found four places that say it is hybrid, including Cornell University, and four seed companies that say it is not. I emailed the company that sold it to me and asked them to tell me once and for all if it is hybrid or not. They never emailed me back. So who knows? There is

One of the hybrid vegetables that fooled the author.

one way to find out for sure—I could hand-pollinate them and then grow them the next year and see if they reproduce true to the parent. But I didn't get around to hand-pollinating these while they were in the bloom stage. So I will no longer have Speckled Hound in my garden.

Purple Haze carrots—I'm really embarrassed about this one. I've been showing these beautiful carrots off and even featuring them in tastings from my garden when I give speeches. I was about to write a whole blog post on them when—lo and behold—I discover on the Internet they are hybrid. The company that sold this seed to me assured me that all of their hybrid seed is marked as such on the packets. But Purple Haze is not marked as hybrid. I've been duped. Erg.

My lesson learned? You have to be very careful who you buy seed from. I only know of three places to buy seed that guarantee their seed is open-pollinated.

The first would be my own seed company, Seed Renaissance.com. I sell guaranteed open-pollinated, non-hybrid, pure heirloom seed, often grown in my backyard garden—and when it's not from my backyard, it's from trusted growers. In addition to garden favorites, I offer some of the very rarest vegetable seed in the world, working to save it from extinction. The other two companies are Seed Savers Exchange and Baker's Creek Seed Company—both worthy and important in their own right.

A "SKILL" WE SHOULD ALL FORGET

There is a so-called "recipe" floating around the Internet, especially on Facebook, that drives me crazy. It's a version of homemade weed killer called "Kill Them All" or some variation of that, and it calls for mixing vinegar and salt together to pour on weeds.

Weed killer indeed.

I've been sounding off about this recipe online for months, at first dismayed and then incredulous as the recipe kept popping up more and more. I belong to several so-called "permaculture" groups that meet online and in person to discuss the concept of permanent sustainable agriculture. Someone on one of these groups posted the recipe for this weed killer. "This is such a bad recipe," I wrote on the comments to the post. "I wish people would stop passing it around,"

"Why?" wrote the person who had posted the recipe.

"Because salt is a permanent decision," I replied. "Gardeners above all others should know this. I don't understand people poisoning their own soil."

"Well, you are trying to poison a plant," responded someone else in the group. "I think it would just

depend on the concentration of salt that ended up on the ground. It's better than what Monsanto gives us to spray."

It's not better, actually. It's not better at all—and if you know me, you know I oppose Monsanto tooth and nail.

"It's hard for me to believe we have to have this discussion on (this permaculture site)," I responded. "Makes me depressed that even gardeners see nothing wrong with salting the earth."

To my surprise, the person who posted the recipe then responded by calling me a "condescending [epithet]."

"Disagreeing with you isn't condescending," I wrote. "I'm genuinely surprised because the whole idea of permaculture is to do no harm."

To which the person responded that I was "arrogant and condescending."

I'm happy to say that several people came to my defense, but I reprint the conversation here because it was eye-opening to me to see how much education there is left to do, even among proponents of "permaculture," which I consider to be the highest form of gardening. (Being called names didn't much bother me—after all, I'm a journalist by trade, and I'd already been called much worse by far more important people on that very day.)

I fear that a lot of people are seeing this weed "solution" and putting it to use. Here's why I think that's a terrible decision:

1. Salt is a permanent decision. If you salt the earth, it will be years before you can use it again. What if you move unexpectedly? (If you don't think people move unexpectedly, you haven't lived very long.) Are you going to walk the next family over to your garden and explain that you salted the earth

for them? What if you decide you need to change things around in your garden? Or what if you read this book and learn that you can have a self-seeding garden, except you have salted between all your garden beds?

2. Let's say that you salt the earth, and three or four years later, something is able to grow in that space again (rejuvenation that soon is possible, depending on how much salt you used). Where do you think all that salt went? Do you think it magically disappeared? I can tell you exactly where the salt went—it headed into the aquifer underground. Or it was captured in runoff and went toward the nearest body of water. In the county where I live, we have a large freshwater lake—a true gem in the middle of the desert. Once upon a time, the south and west shores of the lake were home to groves of commercial fruit trees—until the water in the lake got so salty that it could no longer be used to irrigate the fruit trees. Even alfalfa fields had to be abandoned because of the high salt content on land that was flooded by lake water in the spring. Salt, as I said, is a permanent decision. Once you put it into the ecosystem, it cannot be removed. It can be diluted, and even a decade ago, water managers used to say "the solution to pollution is dilution." They don't say that anymore after it became obvious that dilution ceases to work once the pollution levels grow to a certain tipping point. After that tipping point, the only solutions left often cost hundreds of millions of dollars—and now you know why sewage and run-off fees have jumped so much in the county where I live. Short-sighted solution, long-term natural consequences.

3. Salting the earth was a widespread ancient custom after war—to add famine to injury, the conquering military would salt the land so that the defeated people couldn't grow food to feed themselves. (The Romans used to salt the earth of their enemies, to name one example. There are also examples in the Bible.) Imagine who is laughing when people decide to salt their own earth. The idiocy is astonishing, if you think about it. It certainly proves true the old saying that those who don't learn history are doomed to repeat it.

4. In our society that is flush with morbid obesity—even, and most sadly, among children—why not just get off the couch and pull the weeds? You might need to examine your lifestyle if the only way you can fathom gardening is with a "spray" for every single problem you encounter. I like to call it "going to the gym" when I'm going out to pull weeds. Turn off your television and go get your hands dirty. Go show your kids the value of actual physical work—if you can get your kids away from the video games long enough to see daylight.

5. Now that I've scolded you about spraying weeds, did I mention that I spent five years developing an all-natural, edible weed killer? For some of us with large gardens and pastures, weeding only by hand is not feasible. So I created a "do-no-harm" weed killer. You can read all about it in the "Raised-Bed Gardening" chapter of this book.

6. Finally, here's why the online salt recipe is stupid: If you salt the earth, you don't need any of the other ingredients in the recipe—salt alone will kill the weeds. So if you insist on being stupid, at least be smart about it.

The author, center-right in sunglasses and white shirt, teaches a Forgotten Skills class in his backyard.

CHAPTER 21
BACKYARD RENAISSANCE UNIVERSITY

There is a desperate need for teachers with a living knowledge of homesteading for modern times.

There are so many people who want or need to learn how to be more self-reliant, but they don't know where to start. People long for confidence in their own ability to care for their loved ones, to be frugal, to work with nature and not against her. They crave the independence and freedom that come from practice and home-crafting. They want to show their children by example and be a resource for their neighbors.

Someone recently asked me how they could get started teaching Forgotten Skills classes like mine. I think they wanted me to offer them a certificate or training or some kind of credential to give them credibility. My answer was that they needed to look to their own passions and *teach what they are living*. We need teachers with the expertise of experience. If you have made a skill part of your everyday life and you've been doing it long enough to have failed and learned and then succeeded, your community needs you to teach!

There are myriad topics that could be taught, and should be, but there are a few topics that are desperately, intensely short of teachers qualified to give hands-on classes and demonstrations. These would be:

- Herbal home remedies based on years of experience, not Facebook "recipes"
- The lost art of medicinal poultices
- Cooking with backyard herbs for health and flavor
- Beginning canning and preserving
- Advanced canning and preserving
- Using a pressure cooker (I would pay for this class. I've never used one.)
- Hands-on edible wild foraging and cooking
- Starting a home-based "homestead"-related business
- Starting a homestead handicraft business
- Taxes and accounting for small home businesses

- Online sales and marketing for small businesses
- Fresh pasta making
- Traditional cooking from a century or two ago (why and how)
- Organic gardening
- Organic pest and weed control
- Wellness and family happiness (by someone not looking to sell a product)
- Nurturing children with behavior problems large and small
- Alternative beekeeping (without chemicals, sugar water, or expensive supplies)
- Clean drinking water and water collection for the homestead or emergencies

Forgotten Skills students make winter gardening cold frames in the author's backyard.

- Keeping one or two cows on a small pasture
- Backyard chicken butchering (Be careful advertising that class; just saying.)
- Home apothecary basics
- Advanced home apothecary methods and techniques
- Basketry using only backyard or wildcrafted (not purchased) materials
- Making rugs from fabric scraps (I have tried in vain to even find a rug to buy)
- Milk kefir for beginners
- Water kefir for beginners
- Fermenting vegetables for beginners
- Backyard grain growing
- Beginning homeschooling
- Supplemental homeschooling
- Helping children who are struggling to read or don't seem to love reading
- Wildcrafting medicinal herbs
- Hugelkultur
- Pit composting and slow-posting
- Permaculture
- Purposeful drought gardening
- Advanced seed saving
- Wildcraft seed gathering
- Creating new vegetable varieties
- Stevia cooking
- Kiln-free (Native American) pottery crafting for use and sale
- Small-scale leather tanning

- Nonelectric wood cabinet–making

- Homemade beauty and ablution

- Homemade tooth care and products

- Rustic glassmaking and glasswork

- Vegetable and wildcraft fiber arts

- Vegetable and wildcraft papermaking

- Cob construction basics

- Cob projects: A class where students build one cob project, with supervision

- Reading the natural world: How to interpret meaningful and practical data and signs from clouds, seasons, animals, insects, water, and more.

If you have experience in any of these areas, or if you are willing to teach another nearly forgotten but important skill not listed here, please email me at calebwarnock@yahoo.com. I am always looking for people with a living knowledge of a nearly forgotten skill to co-teach online Forgotten Skills classes with me to a nationwide audience. (I can provide the students and the venue, and you will be paid.) I am also interested in potentially coauthoring books.

BIBLIOGRAPHY

Belliston, N., R. Whitesides, S. Dewey, J. Merritt, and S. Burningham. *Noxious Weed Field Guide to Utah*. Uintah County Weed Department and Utah State University Extension Service, 2010. http://www.utahweed.org/PDF/FieldGuide_Ed4.pdf.

"Bon Arbor Half Inch Cracked-Bone" (advertisement). *Gardeners' Chronicle of America*. (December 1930).

Brill, "Wildman" Steve. "Common Dandelion (*Taraxacum Officinale*)." Accessed September 12, 2013. http://www.wildmanstevebrill.com/Plants.Folder/Dandelion.html.

Carman, John. "The Vegetable Garden." *Gardeners' Chronicle of America* (December 1926).

Centers for Disease Control and Prevention. "Estimates of Foodborne Illness in the United States." Last modified February 6, 2013. http://www.cdc.gov/foodborneburden/.

———. "Personal Preparation and Storage of Safe Water." Last modified May 17, 2013. http://www.cdc.gov/healthywater/emergency/safe_water/personal.html.

Ellis, William S. "Your Work under Glass." *Gardeners' Chronicle of America* (December 1926).

Emerson, Ralph Waldo. "The Rhodora," in *Early Poems of Ralph Waldo Emerson*. New York, 1899. http://www.emersoncentral.com/poems/rhodora.htm.

Fears, Darryl. "Maryland Set to Ban Arsenic-Containing Drug in Chicken Feed." *The Washington Post*, May 20, 2012. http://articles.washingtonpost.com/2012-05-20/national/35455058_1_roxarsone-inorganic-arsenic-tom-hucker.

Germplasm Resources Information Network. "Welcome!" Agriculture Research Service. Last modified April 30, 2013. http://www.ars-grin.gov/.

IBISWorld. "Thrift Stores in the US: Market Research Report." April 2012. http://www.ibisworld.com/industry/thrift-stores.html.

Kallas, John. *Edible Wild Plants.* Layton, UT: Gibbs Smith, 2010.

Nansen, Fridtjof. "The Suffering People of Europe." In *Nobel Lectures, Peace, 1901–1925.* Edited by Frederick W. Haberman. Amsterdam: Elsevier, 1972. http://www.nobelprize.org/nobel_prizes/peace/laureates/1922/nansen-lecture.html.

Project Laundry List. "How much energy is actually used by the clothes dryer?" Accessed September 11, 2013. http://www.laundrylist.org/index.php/faq/35-general-laundry-questions/51--how-much-energy-is-actually-used-by-the-electric-clothes-dryer.

"2012 State of the Industry Report." *Beverage Industry*, July 15, 2012. http://www.bevindustry.com/articles/85663-2012-state-of-the-industry-report?v=preview.

United States Environmental Protection Agency. "Preliminary Risk Assessment for Creosote." Last modified May 9, 2012. http://www.epa.gov/pesticides/factsheets/chemicals/creosote_prelim_risk_assess.htm.

Urban Homestead. "About the Urban Homestead City Farm." Accessed September 12, 2013. http://urbanhomestead.org/about.

Utah Division of Water Rights. "Rainwater Harvesting Registration." Utah.gov. Accessed September 12, 2013. http://waterrights.utah.gov/forms/rainwater.asp.

Wallinga, David. *Playing Chicken: Avoiding Arsenic in Your Meat.* Minneapolis: The Institute for Agriculture and Trade Policy, 2006. http://www.iatp.org/files/421_2_80529.pdf.

Weathers, John. *French Market-Gardening: Including Practical Details of "Intensive Cultivation" for English Growers.* London: J. Murray, 1909. http://archive.org/details/frenchmarketgard00weatrich.

INDEX

D

E

F

G

H

ABOUT THE AUTHOR

Caleb Warnock is the popular author of three nonfiction books and a novel with recipes. He has a master's degree in writing from Utah State University and a bachelor's from Brigham Young University, and he has won more than twenty awards for writing and journalism. Caleb lives with his family on the Wasatch Bench of the Rocky Mountains. He has six stepdaughters and six grandchildren. (There is no *step* between Caleb and his grandchildren.) In his spare time, Caleb relaxes in a hammock strung between an apple and a maple tree, overlooking the perennial flowers and vegetable gardens (yes, he has more than one vegetable garden). His blog, *Backyard Renaissance*, can be found at CalebWarnock.blogspot.com. He sells pure, never-GMO, never-hybrid vegetable seeds (including some of the rarest seeds in the world) at SeedRenaissance.com. You can reach him by email at CalebWarnock@yahoo.com.

HALLIE DOESN'T BELONG in Tippy Canoe, Montana. She's a California girl used to sunshine and warmth—not cold and snow. But after the unexpected death of her estranged husband, she braves the winter weather to wrap up some of his estate details, only to discover that she doesn't fit in and none of the townspeople like her.

THAT IS, except for the town's handsome mayor, who takes quite an interest in Hallie.

BUT WHEN HIS LIFE starts to spiral out of control, she must decide if he's worth sticking around for in the long term. Join Hallie in this fast-paced, hilarious romance as she learns that sometimes love is the only remedy for a broken heart.

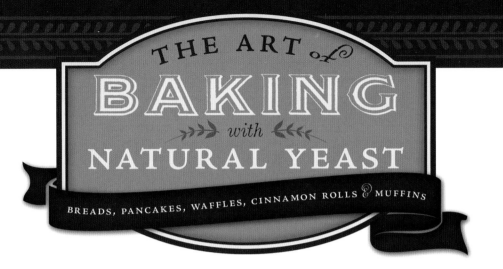
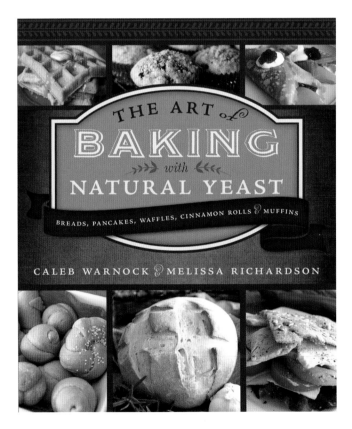

BACKYARD WINTER GARDENING

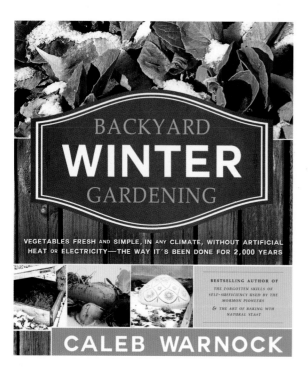

BACKYARD
WINTER
GARDENING

VEGETABLES FRESH AND SIMPLE, IN ANY CLIMATE, WITHOUT ARTIFICIAL
HEAT OR ELECTRICITY—THE WAY IT'S BEEN DONE FOR 2,000 YEARS

BESTSELLING AUTHOR OF
*THE FORGOTTEN SKILLS OF
SELF-SUFFICIENCY USED BY THE
MORMON PIONEERS
& THE ART OF BAKING WITH
NATURAL YEAST*

CALEB WARNOCK

MISCONCEPTIONS ABOUT WINTER GARDENING are everywhere: that it's too difficult, slow, or even impossible. But long before the convenience of grocery stores, people in the 17th, 18th, and 19th centuries used fresh all-natural winter gardening to keep fruits and vegetables on the table even during the coldest months of the year. Feeding your family fresh food from your own backyard garden all winter long is far easier and less time-consuming than you might imagine. And you won't find better-tasting food at any price!

IN BACKYARD WINTER GARDENING YOU'LL LEARN

- how to grow winter produce without electricity, artificial heating, or lighting

- how cold temperatures don't have to result in a dead garden

- how to build a cold frame, a hotbed, and even a geothermal greenhouse for protection from harsh weather

- how children will love vegetables if they take part in the gardening

- how winter gardening protects against economic turmoil, teaches self-providence, and protects your food from unknown chemicals and contamination